# ARARAPÍKVA

## CREATION STORIES
## OF THE PEOPLE

Of related interest from Heyday Books:

**The Way We Lived**
California Indian Stories, Songs & Reminiscences
Edited with commentary by Malcolm Margolin
ISBN 0-930588-55-x, 248 pages, 92 photographs, $14.95

**To the American Indian**
Reminiscences of a Yurok Woman
Lucy Thompson (Che-na-wah Weitch-ah-wah)
ISBN 0-930588-47-9, 322 pages, 25 photographs, $13.95

**The Maidu Indian Myths and Stories of Hanc'ibyjim**
Edited and translated by William Shipley,
foreword by Gary Snyder
ISBN 0-930588-52-5, 192 pages, $12.95

**Flutes of Fire**
Essays on the Languages of Native California
Leanne Hinton
ISBN 0-930588-62-2, 288 pages, $18.00

**News from Native California**
An Inside View of the California Indian World
$4.50 per issue, $17.50 per year

For more information on California Indian history and culture, consider subscribing to this unique and entertaining quarterly magazine. Written and produced by California Indians and those close to the native community, the magazine has lively features and articles on art, ongoing and upcoming events, language, food, traditional skills, political concerns, and more. Beautifully designed, carefully printed, and illustrated with dozens of historical and contemporary photographs, *News from Native California* is not only a source of up-to-the-minute news, but also an important historical archive.

IF THESE TITLES are not available from local bookstores, please send a check in the amount of the cover price plus $1.50 per book for shipping and handling. California residents add sales tax (except for magazines). For a complete list of publications, send $1.00 for our latest catalog. Address all correspondence to **Heyday Books**, P.O. Box 9145, Berkeley, CA, 94709, telephone (510) 549-3564.

# ARARAPÍKVA

CREATION STORIES
OF THE PEOPLE

TRADITIONAL
KARUK INDIAN LITERATURE
FROM
NORTHWESTERN
CALIFORNIA

EDITED AND TRANSLATED BY
JULIAN LANG

HEYDAY BOOKS
BERKELEY, CALIFORNIA

Copyright © 1994 Julian Lang

All rights reserved. No part of this work may be reproduced or transmitted in any form or by any means, electronic or mechanical, including photocopying and recording, or by any information storage or retrieval system, without permission in writing from the publisher, except for brief quotations embodied in critical articles or reviews.

Publisher's Cataloging in Publication
*(Prepared by Quality Books Inc.)*

Ararapikva = Creation stories of the People : traditional Karuk Indian literature from northwestern California / edited and translated by Julian Lang.
   p. cm.
   In English and Karuk.
   ISBN 0-930588-65-7 (pbk.)
   ISBN 0-930588-69-X (hardcover)

   1. Karok Indians--Legends. I. Title: Creation stories of the People.

E99.K25A73 1994                    398.2'04975
                                                 QBI93-22403

Design and Production: Julian Lang and Jeannine Gendar
Cover design: Diana Howard
Cover photo: Dugan Aguilar
Special thanks to LEF Foundation and Friends of *News from Native California*

Published by:   Heyday Books
                      P.O. Box 9145
                      Berkeley, CA 94709

Printed in the United States of America
10 9 8 7 6 5 4 3 2 1

# Dedication

To Indian love.

To the elders:
Elizabeth, Shan, Violet, Fred, Junie, Maggie Joe,
Gram, and Great-gram.

To my family, my son, Jubilee, and my mom.

To all those who refused to deny their identity with and
connection to the Spirit People and the Earth.

To my Karuk language and Karuk belief system.

To the Full Moon.

# Acknowledgements

Special thanks go out to the staff of the Center for Indian Community Development at Humboldt State University in Arcata, California. A number of organizations deserve special mention: the Ink People; (Irahiti) Foundation for Deep Ecology; the Institute of Natural and Cultural Resources; the Kehila Synagogue of Berkeley; the Seventh Generation Fund; and the Tides Foundation.

The wisdom and support of certain individuals have made this book possible. Elizabeth Case and Violet Super, tribal elders, teachers and friends, have supported the efforts of the editor over the years, for which he expresses his deepest thanks. The linguist William Bright's encouragement and generosity contributed to this project immensely. Special thanks go to Doug Tompkins, Jerry Mander, Dagmar Thorpe, Chris Peters, and Tom Sargent.

Lyn Risling has made it all real.

This book is a concept of the Institute of Native Knowledge, a project designed to assert native knowledge and the Fix the Earth belief system.

# Contents

Introduction ..................................................................... 9

Pronunciation Guide ................................................... 32

The Karuk Language .................................................... 34

The Story Tellers .......................................................... 38

Notes on the Translations ........................................... 42

Prayer ............................................................................. 43

How Pishpíshi Got His Stinger ................................... 45

Ikxarámkuusra Muhrôohas—Moon's Wives ............ 49

Eel-with-a-Swollen-Belly Creates Shrines ................ 55

A Trip To Indian Heaven ............................................ 63

What Will Those Who Come After Us Do? .............. 97

Glossary ....................................................................... 102

# Introduction

We call ourselves **áraar**, the People. For generation after generation we have been living in our aboriginal homelands located along the Klamath River in northwestern California. Our land is mountainous, heavily wooded, and is the home of deer, bear, mountain lions, Chinook salmon, steelhead and more. It is the land from which we "sprouted up." It teems with thousands of sacred sites, the geographic locations where creation and spiritual events once occurred at the beginning of time. Not so very long ago our people knew every blade of grass, every creek, mountain and ridge. We knew the origin story of every gravel bar, tree species, animal, bird, insect and body of water.

We call our creation stories **pikva**. The title of this book combines the two words for *people* and *creation story*: **Ararapíkva**—Creation Stories of the People. The collection includes five pieces, each selected to introduce the native knowledge of the Karuk People. The book invites the readers to contemplate a world philosophy, still in practice and born of the natural environment in northwestern California.

## The People

In the "old days," the time before the 1849 invasion of the white gold miners into our country, we lived in villages along the Klamath River, within territory now called the Siskiyou and Salmon Mountains, and the Six Rivers and Klamath National Forests. The villages were situated on the flats and meadows found at the confluences (mouths) of the many creeks feeding the Klamath River and a two-mile stretch up the Salmon River. My people have lived here since the beginning of time.

The age-old social and legal systems which created the sustained peace within our society were mortally disrupted with the arrival of the Americans and Europeans, with their unquenchable thirst for gold. Within two years great epidemics had reduced our population by half. Murders and every form of heinous crime were committed against my ancestors. By 1900 our population was twenty-five percent of our 1849 "first contact" population. Many of the villages

A man in a redwood dugout canoe (**paah**). The canoes were made among the neighboring Yurok, who live downstream of Karuk country. This man is wearing a feathered headdress, with a **pikvas** feather standing up, and a **vaas**, Indian blanket. Photo courtesy of the Smithsonian Institution.

## INTRODUCTION

were burnt down, while others were completely washed away into the river by people using mining technology specifically developed to erode away *our* country; the hydraulic "giants," immense, high-pressure water nozzles, were invented in northern California to swiftly wash away the topsoil to reveal the gold.

The miners considered this their last opportunity for fame and fortune. But, my ancestors experienced an apocalypse as great as the primordial Great Flood had been. The destruction occurring during the first fifty years of contact in northwestern California was as pervasive and horrific as the modern-day nuclear holocaust would have been if it actually had happened. Imagine the physical and psychic destruction and chaos that the otherwise well-governed societies of today would be facing if a nuclear war had occurred during the 1960s or 1970s. The problems caused by the Forty-Niners' thirst for gold at all costs, both human and environmental, are only now beginning to be resolved, one hundred and forty-four years later.

Such wanton destruction causes lasting harm. Some of our most important tribal artists, historians and religious leaders, our ceremonies, villages and sacred lands, were destroyed within twenty years of the first coming of the Americans. Still, our culture has persisted into the present. Many of our ceremonies still occur, both old and new songs are sung, the creation stories are told, and the history of our people continues to be handed down to the young. At this writing we are preparing for numerous dances and ceremonies to Fix the Earth.

Many of the neighboring tribes were not so lucky. Some were wiped out completely, while others fared only a little better. No Indian tribe went unscathed. All experienced incredible mortality rates due to the rampant epidemics of measles, chicken pox, whooping cough, and venereal diseases, the latter most often the result of rape. Our native healers had never seen these illnesses before and knew no remedies. In addition, every American Indian tribe suffered great loss of land and the freedom to live according to native beliefs.

Since the 1880s each successive federal administration has developed policies and created laws to "help" native peoples. Ironically, the help of the liberal and progressive lawmakers has resulted often in further denying native peoples their cultural identity: native languages were outlawed, ceremonies were outlawed, any semblance of the traditional subsistence lifestyle was outlawed. The conquering mentality of the Americans stripped us of our religious objects: the ceremonial regalia and sacred objects were looted. Our common everyday utensils were tagged and boxed up for shipment: the basketry cooking bowls, elkhorn spoons, dugout canoes and our simplest tools. Even the chairs were removed from our houses to be taken away to the Smithsonian Institution! The first fifty years of contact with the Americans by all tribes were rarely, if ever, memorable in any positive sense.

My family did not escape this history. My maternal great-great-grandmother, Polly Conrad, was kidnapped as an adolescent girl in the mid-1860s, removed from her native Wiyot country, on Humboldt Bay, and taken into the mountains as an indentured slave of a German immigrant gold miner. In the late 1840s my paternal great-great-grandfather, **Vaatxarákaan** (of **Vunxarak**), had a dream about "strange, pale people" who were stranded in the snow at a place he recognized high in the mountains. He sent out a search party to rescue what turned out to be some of the first white people to come into our area! My son's generation is

INTRODUCTION

Íchiraay. This man was about 100 years old in 1900. He lived in the Sacred Living House at **Ka'tim'îin.** Bob Offield used to stay with "Old Íchiraay." He said, "I used to like to go stay with him in that old Indian house, and he'd tell me stories that happened maybe three hundred years before *he* was born. Hell, he was over a hundred years old himself. So, I'd go in there and hear stories about what happened four hundred years ago." Photo courtesy of the Smithsonian Institution.

the first of five generations of children in my family *not* to be forced to attend the government-sponsored boarding schools. While these schools taught the three R's, they were designed primarily to undermine the attachment we held for our indigenous religious beliefs, tribal identity and family infrastructure.

The power of love has been instrumental in keeping

Jim Pepper and family, a group portrait. The editor's grandmother's mother was Jim Pepper's younger sister. The dog in the photo is an indigenous **ararachíshii**, Indian dog (considered one of the most sacred animals of the creation). Photo taken in 1898 by John Daggett, courtesy of California State Parks.

indigenous peoples together. Today, many of us, not all, have been raised to love our beliefs and to perpetuate our culture. We have been taught the names of mountains, and heard their creation stories. Some of us were fortunate enough to hear our native languages being spoken in our homes. Many young people now have an opportunity to sing and dance at a Brush Dance ceremony held to heal a sick child, or to participate in our War Dance and White Deerskin Dance in the ceremony to Fix the Earth, called **Írahiv**. And, many do.

In spite of great odds many of our ancestors persisted in being and living according to Karuk beliefs. The concluding

INTRODUCTION

story in this collection is a bittersweet conversation between elder Karuk women in the early 1900s discussing the impact that the "whiteman" society was having upon their world. The speakers asked the looming question: What will those who are born after us do? Today we are asking ourselves a similar question: What does it mean to be a traditional Indian in the last decade of the 20th century?

**How We Lived**
If the reader were to enter a typical village of my ancestors 150 years ago, it would feel and look very different from one of today's small towns. If entering during the day, we would first notice the absence of the men. Most likely, they would be away in the mountains hunting for deer or elk, or fishing at one of the many salmon fisheries along the river. The women, too, would be absent, being out gathering food, basketry materials or the precious iris which was made into Indian string and cordage. The village would be set up in rows of houses, arranged concentrically, one row behind the other. Trails radiated from the village in all directions. Below flowed the ever-present Klamath or Salmon River. The village itself would be located on one of the many flats overlooking the river. The larger the flat, the larger the village. There might be as few as five homes or as many as thirty. What will be noticed is that from every village one is able to see **Ikxariyatúuyship** (God's Mountain), today called Offield Mountain.

The wooden houses had four walls and either a double or single pitched roof. Near to the houses was another wooden structure that looked like a single-pitched roof without walls sitting on the ground. This was the sweat house. Each home was well tended, having a yard and a raised, deck-like porch walled up with smooth, flat, granite flagstones. Long,

Sípnuk'anamahach, "little sípnuk basket." A basket designed to carry treasure. Photo courtesy of the Smithsonian Institution.

forty-foot dugout redwood canoes would be beached at the river's edge. Children might be sitting and working with their elders under the shade of an ancient madrone, ash, or pepperwood (mountain laurel) tree. On the hill above the village we would find the flintery, where the men chipped arrows and other obsidian implements. (It is against Indian law to work obsidian in the house.) If we continued looking we might find a large, flat, pitted stone upon which the women milled their acorns and peppernuts communally.

The evidence of life would be everywhere. Nets of various sizes and strengths would be hung up to dry or for mending. Abundant basketry materials would be sitting about in well-ordered rows: willow and hazel sticks, woodwardia ferns, bear grass and five finger ferns. Fir poles, the implement for gathering sugar pine nuts and other tree foods, protruded from under the eaves of the houses. Frames of the various gathering devices sat about the sweat house and living-house.

Upon entering the living-house, called **ikrívraam**, one would find the fruits of the women's labor. There would be baskets of all kinds and shapes: the immense five-foot high, intricately woven and durable storage baskets, the beautifully designed six-inch high trinket baskets, and other baskets of all shapes and sizes. Each basket would be filled with foodstuffs, treasures, or other objects necessary to maintain the high quality of life that my ancestors enjoyed. There was smoked salmon, deer meat, sturgeon, elk, even prepared bear meat (my tribe was one of the few to eat bear). Every edible plant product was stored in abundance and meticulously. Not seen would be the treasures stored away in carved boxes: the regalia used in the ceremonies.

We are inspired today by the craftsmanship of our ancestors: the featherwork using the brilliant scarlet of the pileated woodpecker, the yellow of meadowlark, hummingbird's ruby, mallard's green, yellowhammer's (flicker's) orange, bluejay's blue, grouse, sparrowhawk and golden eagle's distinctive markings. There were strands upon strands of dentalia, the three- to four-inch, tusk-shaped white shells,

Aráriik, "people place," a Karuk village. Seen is a row of **ikrívraam**, living houses, showing the porches and the protruding ridge poles. This **aráriik** is at **Asánaamkarak**, Ike's Place, located at **Yu'tim'îin**, "downstream-edge-falls," just below **Ka'tim'îin**, "upstream-edge-falls."

ARARAPÍKVA

Above, left: **Ánxuut,** a netted head ornament with painted design and hawk, grouse and bluejay feathers attached. Now called a "hanger," it is worn by the **ikvipvaráyvaansas,** "the ones who go around in the middle," rock packers, the men who pack the obsidian blades in the White Deerskin Dance. Courtesy of the National Museum of the American Indian.

Above, right: **Úhkir,** a wolfskin headband, now called a "blinder." This head ornament is worn by the singer and his two "sidekicks" and assistants in the White Deerskin Dance, which is held during the ceremony to Fix the Earth. Courtesy of the National Museum of the American Indian.

Opposite: **Sipnuk'anamahach, áxak axrúhi, karu vúra íthapathúvriin,** "little sipnuk basket, two elk-horn purses, and just one strand of dentalia." These items were all "money," much sought after and prized. Courtesy of the Smithsonian Institution.

each scrimshawed or wrapped in the iridescent skin of the "money snake" and tipped with a small spray of the woodpecker's scarlet. The dentalia were our currency and were stored away in finely carved and etched elkhorn "purses." The ceremonial dresses were folded away, each being made of two pieces of finely tanned deer hide covered in clam shells, bear grass braiding, juniper berries and chips of abalone shells. Each dress took years to make. Outside the house were buried the thin, finely knapped, six-inch obsidian blades used as money, as well as the giant, thirty-six inch long obsidian blades, pointed at each end and used in the White Deerskin Dance ceremony to Fix the Earth. The decorated otter hide quivers, the dance aprons of ringtail cat, the headbands of timber wolf and the albino deer hides were all carefully stored away in the carved boxes. Some of this regalia was hundreds of years old.

In general shape the living house was similar to today's

single room cabin. The walls were planks, four to eight inches thick, two feet wide and three to six feet high. The roof was held up by two log roof posts (for a single pitched roof) and four runners. The roof was constructed of planks similar to the wall planks. There were no nails (my ancestors had no metal tools), the whole structure being held together by wild grape ropes, cordage, and gravity.

The doors of all the houses were located at the upriver side of the house and faced the river. Each door was round. Crawling through the doorway, one entered onto an earthen ledge running from three to five feet wide that completely encircled the house along the walls. This ledge was where all the baskets and other storage containers were kept, all neatly lined up along the edge and above the six-foot deep, squared-off "sunken living room" located at the center of the living-house. The living room was ten to twelve feet square. One descended into it using a notched ladder located at the front of the house or on the second ladder located at the rear of this semi-subterranean room. The living room (**xavraam**, "house-pit") was the domain of women and the domestic hub of life. During the two meals per day, at daybreak and at sunset, the men entered this house to eat, talk, and decide the important matters concerning the family. Here they decided when to make hunting medicine or go gathering in the mountains, or who would make the prayers for the annual Fix the Earth ceremony.

While the living house was the women's domain, the men spent most of their time together in the sweat house (**ikmaháchraam**). The men slept there. It was also where they made luck. Each man seeking good fortune was required to fast and go up into the mountains before daybreak to gather young fir boughs and return as the sun rose,

INTRODUCTION

Jim Pepper of **Ka'tim'îin** wearing "rich man's clothes," including a headband, called **ikiríkir**, attached with the scarlet head-knots of the pileated woodpecker, and a necklace of dentalia **(ishpukatunvêechas)** worn over one shoulder. He carries an otter hide quiver **(akvákir)** with arrows **(kuníhar)**, a sinew-backed bow **(xúskaamhara)** and a tanned buckskin blanket **(vaas)**. Photo taken in 1898 at **Ka'tim'îin** by John Daggett. Courtesy of the Smithsonian Institution.

wailing and crying for his luck. Everyone in the sweat house was obliged to sweat with the man until the fir boughs were all burnt up.

Some **ikmaháchraam** were small, accommodating five or ten men. Other **ikmaháchraam** were large enough to accommodate twenty or thirty men with ease. The larger villages had more than one sweat house. **Ka'tim'îin**, the village at the Center of the World, had five different sweat houses, as well as the Sacred Sweat House used in the annual ceremony to Fix the Earth. There the men made their hunting medicine, reached decisions regarding marriage, and arranged other legal matters. At night the important male stories were taught to the boys, word by word. Songs were likewise taught. And just as the men were defining the nuance and meaning of Indian law and expressing the ideal way of life in the sweat house, the women were teaching the way of the feminine in the living house. Together these two houses, both considered living entities, were at the center of our culture and identity.

**The Ikxaréeyavs**
**Ikxaréeyav** means God in the People's language, and refers both to our many spirit-deities, and nowadays, to the monotheistic God of modern religions. We have deified everything in the natural world. We consider all of nature to be alive, possessing both feelings and a consciousness. Hence the *natural world* is capable of seeing and hearing us, "blessing" us, and taking pity on us. The Earth is a physical manifestation of God's creative spirit, and we, Human Beings, are recognized by the Earth as a part of the natural world. Once I asked my one hundred and eleven year old great-grandmother, Bessie Tripp, "Who did the old Indians say was God, Grandma?" She said, "Why, the Earth! Ever'thin.' The

## INTRODUCTION

Ôok ithivthaaneen'aachip, "Here at the Center of the World." These are the two ceremonial houses at **Ka'tim'îin** used during the Fix the Earth ceremony. Julian Lang lived just uphill of the sacred sweat house as a child. Photo courtesy of California State Parks.

rocks, the leaves, the mountains." Our sense is that all of nature grows from the Earth as strands of long hair connecting the present with the beginning of time and original knowledge.

Our wisdom tells us that the **Ikxaréeyavs** lived on this world before Human Beings. They grew on this earth-world (as we subsequently were to grow as well). The **Ikxaréeyavs** were hyper-alive, meaning their lives were purely creative. Each moment of their existence resulted in some kind of creation: the realization of a natural law, a powerful song, or a healing herb and medicine formula to cure the gravest ill. The Earth itself was new when they were alive. And, like a new love, every moment, every movement, every idea and feeling was without precedent.

All of the natural world from the earthworm to the mammals, trees, specific geological formations (certain granite outcroppings, for example), sacred sites, mountains, creeks, the sun, the moon, even the mosquito, were once **Ikxaréeyav** People. Each **Ikxaréeyav** experienced an intense and emotional existence. For example, a despised and ill-born man escaped his own murder and was transformed into the moon. Our little sacred mountain, Sugar Loaf (**Á'uuyich**), was once an **Ikxaréeyav** Spirit-man who, being motivated by love, invented all the fishing and hunting tools, and much of our dance regalia. In fact, Sugar Loaf's creative powers resulted in much of what anthropologists call our "material culture." The impressive falls on the Klamath River located at **Ka'tim'îin** (Somes Bar) were created by an enraged **Ikxaréeyav** woman many years ago. Wherever our

**Vuhvúha,** White Deerskin Dance. A line of dancers walks to a dance site at **Ka'tim'îin**, the village located at the Center of the World. The dancers are being led by a "rock packer." Photo courtesy of the Phoebe Apperson Hearst Museum of Anthropology.

INTRODUCTION

ancestors looked or walked in the Karuk world, there was an **Ikxaréeyav** associated with the place.

Zooming around in automobiles or planes today, more and more our perceptions of nature have become abstracted. With each passing day the connection between us (all humanity) and the creation (the natural world) continues to drift further apart. It is easy to overlook the sacredness of the land nowadays, but it's as foolish today as it would have been 150 years ago. It's encouraging to know that our **Ikxaréeyavs** rarely recede into oblivion. After all, are there not yet rattlesnakes? Or frogs, eels, mountains, creeks, trees, and sacred ceremonies? If you look closely enough you'll see they are all **Ikxaréeyavs**.

The most important **Ikxaréeyav** was called **Kahthuxrivishkúruhar**, Upriver Network Sack Carrier. Once Human Beings were settled on the earth he came to inspect the place and institute the Fix the Earth (World Renewal or **Írahiv**) ceremony. First he went to the Konomihu Shasta country up the Salmon River at **Samnâanak**, the Forks of the Salmon, but there were no village areas big enough to accommodate all the World Renewal celebrants. He travelled around the world before establishing the first World Renewal at **Ínaam**, Clear Creek, near present-day Happy Camp, a large village area. He then established an **Írahiv** at **Panámniik**, Orleans, another large village area. **Ka'tim'îin** was next. **Kahthuxrivishkúruhar** then went downriver to the (Algonquian speaking) Yurok people at Weitchpec, and then he went over to the (Athabaskan speaking) Hupa people living on the Trinity River.

**Ithyarukpíhriiv**, Across (the water) Widower, was another very important **Ikxaréeyav**. As they were about to transform and leave this world, he told his son, **Páathkir**, Jump Dance Headdress, "Leave something behind, so

**Yaas'ára**, Human, will have something nice to play with." Thus we have the Jump Dance ceremonial regalia today. All the ceremonies were either established by important **Ikxaréeyavs**, or as is the case with the Brush Dance and Flower Dance, the ceremonies themselves are **Ikxaréeyavs**.

My people celebrated or still celebrate the following ceremonies: the Kick Dance (**piyníknik**), held when a person is going to become a doctor, or when an established doctor becomes ill, primarily a wintertime dance; the Brush Dance (**arara'íhvunaa**, "people dancing"), an herbal medicine dance held for a sick child; and the Flower Dance

**Imvir**, salmon platform fishery, erected at **Asánaamkarak**, "rocky-flat point," Ike's Place. All the fisheries had specific names and were considered personal property. Seen across the river from Ike's is **Ameekyáaraam**, "where they fix the salmon." Photo courtesy of the Phoebe Apperson Hearst Museum of Anthropology.

(**íhuk**), held for the new women of the tribe, the young girls menstruating for the first time.

The last two dances are divine and living beings, **Ikxaréeyav** girls named **Xâapish** (Brush Dance) and **Íhuk** (Flower Dance). They are the first dances to be held in the spring. The Jump Dance follows (called **vuhvuhákaam**, Big-Deerskin Dance), a dance to fix the water and the water spirits and food of our world. Established at **Ameekyáaraam**, "where they fix the salmon," this ceremony is held in the month of July. Finally, the three different Fix the Earth ceremonies are held at the three Karuk spiritual centers mentioned earlier. The first is held during August at **Ínaam**. In early September the second ceremony is held at **Panámniik**. The ceremony begins at **Ka'tim'îin** one day after the **Panámniik** ceremony's conclusion. The ceremonies include War Dances (**thivtaap**) and the Imitation White Deerskin Dance (**vuhvúhiichva**) each year, with the full White Deerskin Dance (**vuhvúha**) every two years. Before 1900, the dances were held according to a schedule devised by the **Ikxaréeyavs**. The first Salmon Ceremony, held in April, initiated the dances. The first salmon of the year, called **ishyâat**, was caught and then was ceremonially cooked, eaten, and the remains cremated. The sacred smoke rose into the heavens, signalling the two **Ikxaréeyav** girl ceremonies, Brush Dance Girl and Flower Dance Girl, to embark on their annual ten-day journey to the Center of the World, bringing back with them the dances for the People.

**Pikváhahirak—Uhyanathêepar**
**Creation Time—Human Time**

Creation stories (**pikva**) chronicle our creation: the origin of the Karuk People and the Karuk World is found in the **pikva**. Some of the stories are told in the exact words of the

**Ikxaréeyav** Spirit People. Many contain instructions for performing certain rituals: the World Renewal ceremony or Brush Dance ceremony. Others contain certain songs: the Peregrine Falcon's song, Bluejay's or Hummingbird's doctoring songs. Still other stories contain secrets about nature: how the Klamath River was created, or why salmon and steelhead run upstream during the spring and fall.

The stories reveal to us that the **Ikxaréeyav** Spirit People loved the Earth and did not want to leave altogether when their time here came to its end. Their job was to learn how to live on this new Earth, to work out the intricacies of life here and unveil the natural laws on behalf of the Human Beings (**Yaas'ára**) who were to follow them. The **Ikxaréeyavs** experienced the range of human emotions: love, hate, longing, passion, fear, contentment, and compassion. When the **Ikxaréeyavs** were told by the Creator to transform, to "go a different way," they left a part of themselves behind for the People here on Earth to remember them by, or they left behind specific knowledge to help Human. The **Ikxaréeyavs** already knew how Human's future was going to be. They left their creation stories behind so we would be able to learn from their wisdom, to learn from their trials.

After the **Ikxaréeyavs** went "a different way," transforming into the trees, herbs, animals and mountains that we now know, *their* stories end. Their era is called **Pikváhahirak**. A new kind of story comes into existence after they leave. They are stories of **Yaas'ára**, the first Human Beings, our ancestors. We call the human-story era **Uhyanathêepar**. These stories are reminders of the goodness that comes when Humans rely on the spirit of the Earth and believe in the **Ikxaréeyavs'** words. We are told of the hardships that must be undergone in order to receive the power, luck or the pity that only the Earth, the mountains, and the **Ikxaréeyavs**

**Tá kunvuhvúhinaati**, they are dancing the White Deerskin Dance. The white deerskins (**púfichtaahkoo**) are held out, "while they feed." One can see the regalia of the dance, the tall feathers, the wolfskin blinders, the necklaces, the ringtail cat dance aprons, and the deerskins with the woodpecker scalps decorating their eyes, ears, legs and mouths. This photo was taken at a **Panámniik** World Renewal Ceremony. Photo courtesy of the National Museum of the American Indian.

can bestow upon the people. Many of the stories tell of love, or about gaining wealth through spiritual acts, while others tell of the dark side: sorcery, war, and revenge.

Both kinds of stories, stories of the **Ikxaréeyavs** and of **Yaas'ára**, are considered to be living entities. They have an existence unto themselves, being a part of the creation like the trees, the animals, and the mountains. Accordingly, we are responsible to regard them with the utmost respect, taking care not to abuse them.

Wintertime was storytelling time. Bad luck would follow

anyone who told stories at the wrong time. The prime storytelling place was the **ikrívraam**, the living house. After dinner somebody said, "**Chimi nupikváhi!**" "Let's tell creation stories!" Everyone sat around the fire as the family **pikváhaansas**, storytellers, or guests told their favorite **pikva** well into the night.

A story often begins with the word "**uknîi**." There is no meaning except to announce that a story is about to begin. After this word has been spoken no one present can interrupt, ask questions or interfere in any way with the storytelling, because the story is alive, its power is invoked, and once started it must be told from its beginning to its end. If the storyteller forgets a passage, he or she must start the story again. The word **Kupánakanakana** is said when the story ends. A short prayer is then said to beckon the bountiful foods and good times of the upcoming spring months. Finally, someone in the house will say, "**Chimi núkviithi!**" "Let's go to sleep!" Then the men return to their sweat house, while the women go to sleep in the **ikrívraam**.

Learning the creation stories was quite an ordeal, since they had to be learned verbatim. The student, the young girl or boy, would listen to the story and then recite it back to his or her teacher word for word, until able to tell the whole story. The process usually took all night and often took days to complete, if the story was long and complex. It was an important learning process because the stories became the basis for medicine-making among our people. Herb doctors, the Brush Dance Doctor for instance, gather and then "talk to" the plants—that is, he or she recites a creation story, called a formula, over the herbs. Only then are they considered medicine. For us the healing spirit is not of the present. The spiritual power that invigorates the healing process is always ancient, and always from the creation

INTRODUCTION

**Ka'tim'îin**, looking upstream. Across the river is the village site of **Ishipíshrihak**, Phoebe Maddux's home village. The photo shows both whiteman and Karuk houses. The Center of the World is one of the most populated places along the Klamath River. Note the open, brush-free hillsides when this photo was taken. Since then, U.S. Forest Service policies have resulted in the hillsides being covered with nearly impenetrable brush here and throughout the countryside. The two houses at the edge of the flat are the same ones shown in the photo on page 23. Courtesy of California State Parks.

times. The stories are essential to release the healing medicines of the earth.

The first four selections included herein are stories from the earliest times. They are about the **Ikxaréeyavs**, the Spirit People, or about **Yaas'ára**, the first Human Beings. They are branches of a vast tree of native knowledge with roots extending deep into the past and future.

> Julian Lang
> **Ithivthaanéen'aachip vákuusrah**
> Center of the World moon
> September 1993
> Eureka, California

# Pronunciation Guide

Within the old Karuk tradition, **pikva** stories are handed down orally. Very important qualities of the **pikva** are brought out when they are recited aloud: their power to evoke ethos and pathos.

The following guide is designed to help you begin voicing the language from the Center of the World. Remember to pronounce each of the five vowels and sixteen consonants distinctly. Pay special attention to the difference between long and short vowels. And, speak slowly. Fluent elder Grace Davis once gave this advice: "People can understand when you pronounce your words slowly."

## VOWELS

a    short vowel; as in f*a*ther. **áka**, father.
aa    long vowel; as in the exclamation *aa*h. **akraa**, eel.
ee    long vowel; as in h*ay*. **éepaax**, alder bark.
i    short vowel; as in *it is*. **upíti**, he is saying.
ii    long vowel; as in *ee*l; **íinva**, forest fire.
oo    long vowel; as in H*o*mer. **anoo**, ouch!
u    short vowel; as in b*oo*t. **múmuh**, dull.
uu    long vowel; as in wh*o*? **púuk**, fog.

## CONSONANTS

ch    as in *ch*ur*ch*; **chánchaaf**, foam.
f    as in *f*an; **fáath**, manzanita.
h    as in *h*ot; **hámi**, isn't that so?
k    as in *k*oo*k*; **kachakâach**, bluejay.
m    as in *m*om; **múmuh**, dull.
n    as in *n*o; **náa**, I.
p    as in *p*ipe; **ípih**, bone.

## PRONUNCIATION GUIDE

r   is trilled, like the Spanish r in to*r*o; **kúrat**, California woodpecker.
s   as in *s*auce; **símsiim**, knife.
sh   as in *sh*ow; **íshaha**, water.
t   as in *t*ote; **táat**, mother.
th   as in au*th*or; **thivtaap**, War Dance.
v   is pronounced by placing the upper and lower lips together, instead of placing the upper teeth on the lower lips; **ávaha**, food.
x   as in the German word a*ch*; **xára**, a long time.
y   as in bo*y*; **yâamach**, pretty.
'   The apostrophe indicates a glottal stop, as in the exclamation "oh-oh!" when used before a vowel; **kumá'ii**, because.

### INTONATION

The musical quality of every language is the result of the rising and falling of tones, the staccato of the consonants, all combined with personal speaking style. The stress and pitch of words written in the Karuk language is aided by the following accent marks:

´   Acute accent indicates a stressed syllable as in: **amáyav**, good tasting; **ápsuun**, snake.
^   Circumflex accent indicates a rising-falling tone: **îikam**, outdoors; **ihrôoha**, wife.
~   Tilde indicates a nasalized vowel as in: **hãa**, yes; **hãa'ii**, exclamation of annoyance.

The following example is a typically accented sentence in the Karuk language:

Pihnêefich vaa ukúphaanik. Panámniik u'ífanik.
Coyote thus he-did. Orleans he-was-raised.
*Coyote did that. He was raised at Orleans.*

# The Karuk Language

The Karuk language is considered by linguists to be a member of the Hokan family of American Indian languages. It is distantly related to other languages such as that of the Shasta (the neighbors to the east), various Pomo languages of central California, and the Yuman languages of southern California and Arizona. These languages are no more mutually comprehensible than English, Russian, Italian, and Sanskrit, all members of the Indo-European language family.

The Karuk language was being spoken by an estimated 2,000 people at the time of the Gold Rush. By the early 1970s there were only about 150 fluent speakers left. Today there are fewer than a dozen, although people are seeking to reverse this cataclysmic decline through language programs and a variety of grass roots efforts.

The following notes are presented to give the reader a very rough outline of a few aspects of Karuk grammar.

**I. Pronouns used as prefixes:**

| | |
|---|---|
| na- | I |
| i- | you (singular) |
| u- | he, she, it |
| nu- | we |
| ku- | you (dual plural) |
| kun- | they |

**II. Independent pronoun forms:**

| | |
|---|---|
| náa | I |
| íim | you (singular) |
| úum | he, she, it |
| núu | we |

iimkun you (dual plural)
uumkun they

## III. Verbs

A regular verb construction essentially contains three parts: the subject, the verb stem, and the third part, which contains the number, the directional suffixes, and/or the verb tense. The following sentences will help illustrate this.

Pihnêefich vaa ukúphaanik.
Coyote that he-did-anciently.
*Coyote did thus.*

Panámniik u'ífanik.
Orleans he-was-raised-anciently.
*He was raised at Orleans.*

In the first sentence the verb phrase, ukúphaanik, is constructed in this manner: u- (he) is the subject, -kúpha- is the verb stem (infinitive: kúupha, to do), and -anik indicates the ancient past tense.

In the second sentence u- is the subject, -íf- is the verb stem, and -anik indicates the ancient past tense.

The verb in the following sentence illustrates number as well as tense.

Vaa káan pakuntáxraatvanaatihanik.
Thus there they-were-chipping-obsidian-anciently.
*Long ago they were chipping obsidian there.*

The verb phrase, pakuntáxraatvanaatihanik, consists of the following elements:

| | |
|---|---|
| pa+kun- | subject (they) |
| -táxraat- | verb (to work arrowheads) |
| -vanaa- | plural ending |
| -tih- | durative tense |
| -anik | ancient past tense. |

The following verb phrases contain directionals:

utrôovuti
he-looks-upriverwards
*he looks upstream*

| u- | subject (he) |
| -it- | verb (to look) |
| -rôovu- | directional (upriverwards) |
| -ti | durative tense |

upikfúkuvraa
he-crested-over (a mountain or ridge)
*he crested the ridge*

| u- | subject (he) |
| -pikfúku- | verb (to crawl, walk in mountains) |
| -vraa | directional (over) |

The future tense is formed by adding -heesh to the subject and verb stem.

ni'axaychákishriheesh
I-am-going-to-grab-her
*I am going to grab it*

| ni- | subject (I) |
| axaychákishrih- | verb (to grab) |
| -heesh | future tense. |

There are several other past tenses, and there is a present tense used commonly in normal conversation and often in stories as well.

Verbs indicate the number of subjects: singular, dual (i.e. two subjects) and plural (three or more subjects). Some verbs change dramatically when the subject number changes.

For instance,

    **níkrii**             I live
    **nu'iin**            we-two live
    **nu'áraarahiti**   we (many) live

### IV. Nouns

The definite article is the prefix pa- (the). There is no indefinite article (a, an).

Nouns are pluralized in their regular form by adding -sa, -s, or -sas.

    **asiktávaan**, woman; **asiktávaan**s**as**, women
    **ávansa**, man; **ávansa**s, men.

There are other, less-used forms:

    **ifápiit**, young lady; **ifápiit**s*h*a*s*, young ladies
    **típah**, brother; **tipáh***iivsh**as**, brothers.

Adjectives and adverbs are often affixed to the noun.

    **ikrivrámtaay**, literally house-lots, meaning lots of houses.
    **ithkaxára**, feather-long, i.e. the eagle plumes used in the Deerskin Dance.

# The Storytellers

**Phoebe Maddux.** Photo courtesy of the Center for Indian Community Development, Humboldt State University.

**"How Pishpíshi Got His Stinger" and "Moon's Wives":** Phoebe Maddux was born and raised at **Íshipishi**, the village located across river from **Ka'tim'íin**. Her Indian name was **Imkánvaan**, "wild sunflower gatherer." Phoebe Maddux single-handedly helped save vast amounts of Karuk native knowledge through her extensive (more than five years) consultation with John P. Harrington, a linguist working with the Bureau of American Ethnology. Maddux often consulted with elders still living during the mid-1920s, learning songs, specific stories, medicine formulas, and other cultural information. She then transmitted them to

Harrington. I'd like to invent an award, the Order of the Mountains, perhaps, and bestow it on Phoebe Maddux for her effort and heart.

**Fritz Hansen.** Photo courtesy of the National Archives.

**"Eel-with-a-Swollen-Belly Creates Shrines":**
Fritz Hansen was renowned as a singer of White Deerskin Dance songs, and a composer of Kick Dance songs. He had two Indian names, **Afrîich** and **Chaakíchhaan**. Originally of **Ka'tim'îin**, he was an authority on the Fix the Earth ceremony, although he never performed as the **fatavêenaan**, or priest, of the ceremony. Elders today remember Fritz well. All like to tell stories of his little store at **Ka'tim'îin** where he always gave the kids a piece of candy.

**"A Trip to Indian Heaven":**
Margaret Harrie (née Albers) was from **Íramnihirak** (Irving

**Margaret Harrie.** Photo courtesy of Elizabeth Uldall.

Creek). Her Indian name was **Mâakich**, a Karukacized form of the English name Maggie. She was the mother of Benonie Harrie, the highly regarded Indian doctor (**êem**), and was living at Quartz Valley at the time this story was collected.

**"What Will Those Who Come After Us Do?"**
The speakers of this piece are unknown, although surely they were some of the oldest women of the tribe.

**SOURCES**
**Pishpíshi, Moon's Wives** and **Eel-with-a-Swollen-Belly:** The Papers of John P. Harrington. National Archives. All were collected in 1926.

**Indian Heaven:** Hans Jørgen Uldall, U.C. Berkeley, Survey of California and Other Indian Languages archives. Collected in 1932.

**What Will Those Who Come After Us Do?**
"Tobacco Among the Karok Indians of Northwestern California," John P. Harrington, Bureau of American Ethnology, adapted by Julian Lang.

The first four stories have not been published until now. When he collected the first three stories, Harrington included a general translation of the texts without interlinear (literal) texts. The fourth story was recorded entirely in phonetic form by Hans Jørgen Uldall. The final story was published without interlinear texts by the Bureau of American Ethnology in "Tobacco Among the Karuk Indians of California," by John Harrington. For *Ararapíkva,* the Harrington and Uldall phonetic transcriptions were transferred into the Karuk practical spelling system, a writing system currently in use and adopted by the Karuk Language Restoration Committee of the Tribal Council of the Karuk Tribe of California. The editor developed full English translations for all of the pieces.

# Notes on the Translations

Those who have learned another language know the experience of having to think differently when translating ideas from one language to another. *Ararapíkva* offers the reader the opportunity to see and experience an indigenous California way of thinking and relating to the world. In the Karuk language the earth, the environment, the bioregion, is called **ithívthaaneen**, laying-around. The word for sky is **páy nanu'ávahkam**, that above-us. Mount Shasta is **Úytaahkoo**, white-mountain. The moon is called **ikxarámkuusra**, dark-sun.

The idea behind this book is to introduce an indigenous way of thought. World-views are defined by languages. The primary objective of *Ararapíkva* is to share a cultural experience, not to present a scholarly monograph or journal article.

The first line of the story text contains the Karuk language. The second line is the Karuk story literally translated into English. The third line (in italics) is the English adaptation of the story.

# Prayer
## Spoken At End of Creation Stories

*Chéemyaach ík Ishyâat*
*imshiríhraavish!*
*Náyaavheesh ik!*
*Chéemyaach ík Ataychúkinach*
*i'uunúpraveesh!*
*Náyaavheesh ik!*
*Nanivási vúra veekinayâach!*


*Hurry and flash upstream Spring*
  *Salmon!*
*You must hurry!*
*Hurry and sprout up young*
  *brodiaea!*
*You must hurry!*
*My back is straight!*

# How Pishpíshi Got His Stinger

This is a story of the **Ikxaréeyavs** before the transformation. **Pishpíshi**, yellowjacket, is a member of the fierce, **ishímfir** (hot-fleshed), poisonous ones who are gathered on Mount Shasta to make the weapons with which they will hurt human beings in the world to come.

The story might be seen as an explanation of how it is that yellowjackets sting, and why their sting is less painful than that of rattlesnakes or scorpions. More than that, though, the story foreshadows "medicine." When a child is stung, a medicine formula version of the story is recited, to take away the pain. The formula concludes with the phrase: *Iim mí'if ni'aapúnmuti, pishpíshi:* "I know how you were raised, yellowjacket." Knowledge, which is what the story is, gives power.

## ARARAPÍKVA

Vaa káan pakuntáxraatvanaatihanik,
Thus there they-were-chipping-obsidian-anciently,
*Long ago they were chipping obsidian there,*

    koovúra pakáan kuntáxraatvanaatihanik Úytaahkoo.
    all who-there they-were-chipping-obsidian mountain-white.
    *they were all making their obsidian arrowheads there at Mount Shasta.*

Koovúra pakêemishas pakóo ára píipvanaatihansan,
All the-bad-ones that-all people ones-who-sting,
*They were all the monstrous and mean animals who would be stinging people in the future,*

    vaa kumakêemishas.
    that kind-of-bad-ones.
    *those kinds of vicious beings.*

Vaa uumkun koovúra pakáan kuntáxraatvanaatihanik.
That they all who-there they-were-chipping-obsidian-arrowheads-anciently.
*They were all making obsidian arrowheads there at Mount Shasta long ago.*

Vaa kunipítihanik, "Vaa mûuk Yáas'ára
That they-said-anciently, "That by-means-of, Humans
*They were telling each other how they would be*

nuykáratiheesh, pananúsaak mûuk."
we-will-kill, our-obsidian-arrowheads by-means-of."
*killing human beings with their arrowheads (in the future).*

Ápsuun pa'ishimfiréeshiiphanik músaak.
Snake the-fiercest was his-arrowhead.
*Rattlesnake's obsidian point was the deadliest.*

Mahxánthuun káru pa'ishímfir pamúsaak.
Uphill-crawfish too as-strong his-arrowhead.
*Scorpion's arrowhead was also deadly.*

Víri vaa uum káru pishpíshi u'ífiktihanik
So that he too yellowjacket he-picked-them-up-anciently
*Yellowjacket was there, too, picking up*

    pásaak pataxrátraam.
    the-obsidian-points the-flintery.
    *little obsidian flakes at the arrowhead workplace.*

Vúra pufáathara tûupichas u'ífiktihanik pásaak.
Just nothing little-ones he-picked-up-anciently arrowheads.
*The arrowheads he was picking up were little obsidian flakes amounting to nothing.*

Kóomahich vúra poomfírahiti pishpíshi.
A-little-while just it-pains yellowjacket.
*So, nowadays yellowjacket's arrowheads hurt for just a little while.*

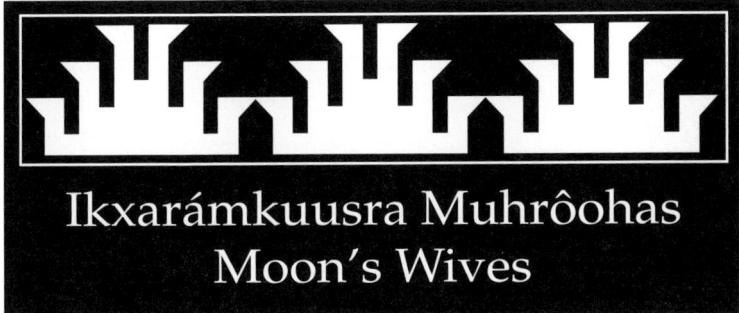

# Ikxarámkuusra Muhrôohas
# Moon's Wives

**Pay nanu'ávahkam áhootihaan,** Skywalker, is one of the names for Moon. He has three wives: Frog, Grizzly Bear, and Rattlesnake. All three can be seen on his surface during a full moon.

In the Karuk world, the moon is not an inanimate object, some huge dead rock. Far from it—he and his wives are divine, Ikxaréeyavs, still visible to us all. And they are motivated not by the laws of physics, nor by an abstract set of religious principles, but rather by what motivates all living things: lust, passion, deeply felt and sometimes mysterious yearnings. Frog Woman is drawn toward the moon, hoping to become his best wife. We live in a world created by yearning and sexuality, and every time we look at the moon and see Frog Woman there, we are reminded of this wonderful fact.

## ARARAPÍKVA

Uum vúra xára vúra tutáapkuupanik, pay nanu'ávahkam áhootihanik.
She just a-long-time just she-liked him-anciently, this us-above walked-anciently.
*It seems she had liked Moon, the-one-who-walks-in-the-sky, for a very long time.*

Xás vúra uum táyaan pooxúsaanik, "Chími nishôomkireesh."
Then just she lots-of-times that-she-was-thinking, "I-am-going-to-go-offer-myself-in-marriage."
*Many, many times she thought she would offer herself in marriage to Moon.*

Xás itháan uxús, "Chími kanvâarami!"
Then once she-thinks, "I-am-going-there!"
*Once she thought, "I'm going to go to him!"*

Xás papishîich ukfúkuvraanik xás upiip,
Then the-first she-climbed-to-the-crest-of-the-ridge then she-said,
*When she arrived at the top of the first ridge, she said,*

"Mánik kúnish ûumukich póokrii."
"Seems sort-of close-by where-he-lives."
*"The Moon's place seems so close (that I'll be seeing him in no time)."*

Xás u'áhoonik.
Then she-walked-in-ancient-times.
*Then, she started walking.*

Yíthuk kúna kumáviitkir tóoskakathva.
At-some-other-place different its-ridge she-jumps-across.
*Then she jumped across to the next mountain ridge.*

Tóopiip, "Vúra kúnish chími ni'áfisheesh,
She-said, "Just sort-of I-am-going-to-touch-it,
*(There on the new ridge) she said, "It feels as if I'm just about to touch his house,*

    kóova ûumukich kunish póokrii."
    so-all close-by sort-of where he-lives."
    *it's so close by."*

Xás vaa káan pooskáaksipreenik, ithyarukirá viitkir xás uskákishrihanik.
Then that there where-she-jumped-from-anciently, across ridge then she-jumped.
*Then she jumped from the mountain ridge top there, jumping across to the next ridge.*

Kay kúkuum tu'ípahoo.
Again she-travelled.
*She kept on travelling in this way.*

ARARAPÍKVA

Kúkuum vúra vaa tóokuupha.
Again just that she-did.
*She did the same thing as before (jumping from ridge to ridge).*

Kúkuum vúra vaa tóoxus, "Chími ni'áfisheesh."
Again just that she-thought, "I-am-about-to-touch-it."
*And again she thought, "It's as if I can touch the Moon from this ridge."*

Pavíitkir patookfúkuvraa kúkuum, kúkuum ík vúra púxay vúra.
The-ridge that-she-crested again, again must just not-at-all just.
*When she made it up to the next ridge, still she was not yet to the Moon.*

Káruma ník vóokupiti, pooxúvraan ithyarukirá viitkir xás tooskákish.
The-fact-is yet that-she-was-doing, where-there-were-hollows across ridge then already-jumped-to.
*The fact is, she had been jumping from ridge to ridge across all the hollows and gulches.*

"Vúra ni'úumeesh."
"Just I-am-going-to-arrive."
*She kept thinking, "I am just about to arrive at Moon's house."*

## IKXARÁMKUUSRA

Táyaan poopikyaavárihvanik.
Lots-of-times that-she-tried.
*She tried to get to Moon many different times.*

Táyaan vúra uparatánmaahpanik.
Lots-of-times just she-turned-back-from-her-journey.
*She had turned and gone back home many times already.*

Chavúra u'úumanik.
Finally she-arrived.
*Finally, she arrived at Moon's house.*

Payêem vúra vaa káan upáthyuuxriv Pakúusra
mukrívraam ithyúukiruk.
Now just that there she-sat-with-her-legs-sticking-
straight-out-in-front-of-her the-Moon his-house one-side-
of-the-house.
*And so now, she sits in Moon's house, to one side of the house,
with her legs sticking straight out in front of her.*

Ihroohéeshiip.
Wife-best.
*She was Moon's best wife.*

Uum uxúti, "Naa ihroohéeshiip."
She she-was-thinking, "I best-wife."
*She thought, "I am the best wife."*

## ARARAPÍKVA

Kúyraak pamuhrôohas Pakúusra.
Three his-wives the-Moon.
*The Moon has three wives.*

Xanchíifich, ithyûukirukam vúra pachéech poopáthyuuxti,
Frog, one-side-of-the-house just alone that-she-sits-with-legs-straight-out,
*In the full moon Frog is the one who sits alone and to one side with her legs sticking straight out,*

> xás ithyûukirukam vúra takun'ífchuy.
> then the-side-of-the-house just already-they-crowded.
> *while the other wives sit crowded at the other side of the house.*

Pirishkâarim uum káru kêech pa'asiktávaan.
Grizzly-bear she also big the-woman.
*His wife, Grizzly Bear, is a big woman, too. (As big as Frog.)*

Káru uum, Tapas'ápsuun, nîinamich vúra pa'asiktavanxára.
And she, Real-snake, small just woman-long.
*Rattlesnake is a long, slender woman.*

Yôoram vúra póokrii, Tapas'ápsuun.
In-the-back-of-the-house, Real-snake.
*Rattlesnake stays in the back of Moon's house.*

Vaa kunípeenti, vaa áta peehroohéeshiiphanik yôoram póokrii.
That they-say, that perhaps the-best-wife-anciently in-the-back-of-the-house that-she-lived.
*The old people used to say that Moon's best wife was the one who lived in the back of the house: Rattlesnake.*

# Eel-with-a-Swollen-Belly Creates Shrines

Eel-with-a-Swollen-Belly, the Ikxaréeyav who became the lamprey eel, may seem like the most peculiar of beings. But to us, he too is divine, man-like in his shape in this story, which takes place just before the great transformation.

Although apparently simple, this story of Eel-with-a-Swollen-Belly travelling along the Klamath River and piling rocks into shrines is layered with complexity, with things upon which one can meditate and dwell. The movement of this Ikxaréeyav up and down the river foreshadows the migration of eels in the world today. By stopping at various places along the Klamath River, he endows these places with the sanctity of myth. His building of shrines sets the example for what humans must do even today. The building of shrines connects us, mysteriously, with the times and spirit of the Ikxaréeyavs.

Is Eel-with-a-Swollen-Belly a god, a man, or a fish? Why does he build these shrines? There are so many questions that modern people would like to have answered with clarity. But does everything in this world have to have an easy answer? Can it be that we need wonder and mystery more than we need answers? Perhaps one of the reasons that the Ikxaréeyavs left these precious stories was to remind us that wonder is at the heart of creation.

## ARARAPÍKVA

Uknîi.
*I am going to tell a creation story.*

Ataháriva kun'áraarahitihanik.
At-one-time they-were-living-in-ancient-times.
*People were living here in ancient times.*

Aknahvishvan'ímxuupanach úum yúruk ithivthaneen 'ífuthkam u'ífanik.
Eel-belly-swollen-little he downriver [at] world behind-side he-grew-up-in-ancient-times.
*The man named Eel-with-a-Swollen-Belly grew up at the downstream end of the world in the earliest days.*

Vaa káan pamu'áka mukrívraamhanik, yúruk ithivthaneen'ífuthkam.
That there his-father his-living-house-in-ancient-times, downstream world-behind-side.
*Eel was raised at his father's house there at the downstream end of the world.*

Pamútaat káruk ithivthaneen'ípan va'árahanik.
His-mother upriver world-end its-person-in-ancient-time.
*His mother belonged to the people who lived at the upriver edge of the world.*

Kári xás uxúsaanik,
And then he-thought,
*And then Eel thought,*

## AKNAHVISHVAN'ÍMXUUPANACH

"Nanivápuhirak chími kanipvâarami."
"My-mother's-birthplace may-I-go-home."
*"I want to go home to the place where my mother was born and raised."*

Víri vaa poo'árihraatihanik,
So that as-he-travelled-up,
*As he was travelling along upstream,*

> kôokaninay vúra kumeenirahíram póoyriivshamtihanik.
> every-place just its-living-place that-he-made-his-shrinepiles-in-ancient-times.
> *he started piling rocks and making shrines at every place where humans were going to be living.*

Xás vaa tóopiip, "Yaas'ára'îin napikrôoktiheesh ôok pay.
Then that already-he-said, "Humanity-by-them they-are-going-to-remember-me here.
*About this piling of rock Eel said, "This place here is where human will remember me.*

> Vaa pay'ôok ás utháantakutiheesh."
> That here stone he-will-put-it-on-in."
> *They will remember me and will place a rock here on the shrine pile."*

Pa'ôok ithivthanéen'aachip poo'áhoonik,
The-here earth-middle where-he-travelled-in-ancient-times,
*When Eel travelled through the Center of the World place here,*

## ARARAPÍKVA

víri ôok ithivthanéen'aachip xás pávaa ukúphaanik,
so here earth-middle then the-that he-did,
*he did something different,*

xakararáastiip, vúra úyriivshavanik.
both-sides-river's-edge, just he-piled-rocks-in-ancient-times.
*he made the rock-shrines on both sides of the Klamath River.*

Uxúsaanik, "Ôok vaa páy táay kunifyúkutiheesh Yaas'ára.
He-thought, "Here that this lots they-will-be-walking-around Humanity.
*He was thinking, "There will be many people travelling around here at the Center of the World.*

Víri vaa pay'ôok kanapikrôoktiheesh pakuníyrivshaamtiheesh.
So that right-here they-will-remember-me when-they-pile-rocks-on-the-shrine.
*In this way the future people can remember me by placing a stone on the shrine here.*

Tákunpiip, 'Matêe xára nímyaahtiheesh.'"
Already-they-say, 'Let-it-be long-time I-am-going-to-be-living.'"
*The future-humans will say, 'May I live a long time,' (as they place their shrine-stone)."*

Xás vúra vaa u'áhootihanik.
Then just that-he-travelled-in-ancient-times.
*And Eel travelled on in this way.*

## AKNAHVISHVAN'ÍMXUUPANACH

Vaa vúra u'ahóokiritihanik peeshkéesh.
Then just he-travelled-by-means-of the-Klamath-River.
*The Klamath River was his guide as he travelled upstreamward.*

Usaamváraktihanik.
It-flowed-downstreamwards-in-the-ancient-times.
*The river flowed down from the upriver end of the world.*

Xás kúkuum vaa káan upíyriivshavanik Ínaam, poo'áhootihanik.
Then again that there he-placed-an-offering-in-ancient-times Inaam (Clear Creek), as-he-was-walking-in-ancient-times.
*He made another shrine as he travelled, there at the Inaam World Renewal site.*

Kúkuum vúra vaa káan váa úpaanik,
Again just that there that he-said,
*At Inaam he repeated his words from before,*

"Ôok pay Yaas'ára'îin napikrôoktiheesh."
"Here this Humanity-by I-am-going to-be-remembered."
*"At this place here Human will remember me."*

Víri payêem vúra vaa kunpikrôokti.
So now just that they-remember-him.
*So, now Human remembers Eel in that way (by placing rocks on the shrines).*

## ARARAPÍKVA

tKúkuum vaa káan uparámsiipreenik, kúkuum u'ípahoonik.
Again that there he-came-from, again he-continued-travelling.
*He started out from Inaam as he had in all the village-sites before, and continued travelling upstream.*

Chavúra káruk ithivthaneen'ípan u'úumanik,
Finally upstream world-end he-arrived,
*Finally he reached the upriver end of the world,*

    muvápuhirak u'íipmanik.
    his-mother's-birthplace he-went-back-there.
    *arriving at his mother's birthplace.*

Vaa káan xás pakraah upárihishrihanik.
That there then the-lamprey-eel he-transformed-into-in-ancient-times.
*And that's where he transformed into the lamprey eel we know today.*

Itháan uum ávansahanik.
Once he man-in-ancient-times.
*Eel was once a man long ago.*

Víri vaa uum káan xás pakraah upárihishrihanik.
So that he there then the-eel he-transformed-into.
*And, that's the way he transformed into the lamprey eel at the upriver end of the world.*

## AKNAHVISHVAN'ÍMXUUPANACH

Aknahvishvan'ímxuupanach vaa ukúphaanik,
Eel-belly-swollen-little that-he-did-in-ancient-times.
*Eel-with-a-Swollen-Belly did this long ago.*

Kupánakanakana.
*The myth is over.*

# A Trip To Indian Heaven

This story gives us knowledge about **Arutâanahitihirak**, the region we call "Indian heaven." The story reminds us, for example, that there are two paths indicated on **yumaréempaah** (dead person's path), the Milky Way. The left fork is for the common people to travel on and the right path is for "good" people, those who attend the **Írahiv**, the Fix the Earth ceremonies.

A major purpose of this story is to explain and ordain the use of angelica root, **kíshvuuf**, our most powerful medicine. Angelica can make our bones grow back when death invades our lives. It makes us strong. Weaving baskets and singing are two other ways of making our bones come back when we feel so bad because of a loved one's passing.

This is also a love story. The affirmation of love as the greatest force on earth is balanced by the knowledge that even love has its limits: life must be lived according to the rules that have been laid down for us.

# ARARAPÍKVA

Uknîi.
*I am going to tell a creation story.*

Káan áraar kun'áraarahiti.
There people they-were-living.
*In our ancient times a particular family was living in our world.*

Ifápiit kunthíinati.
Young-girl they-had.
*These people had a young girl.*

Chavúra tá xára xasík keechíkyav uthíinati, pamukun 'ifápiit.
Finally already a-long-time then sweetheart she-had, their-young-girl.
*After a long time had passed, their girl was in love and had a sweetheart.*

Chavúra tá pâanpay, axmáy vúra puyáv ipmahóonkoonara.
Finally already after-awhile, suddenly just not-good she-is-feeling.
*As time passed on, suddenly the girl fell ill.*

Xás pa'ávansaník xuus u'éethti pamukeechíkyav.
Then the-man yet he-took-care-of-her his-sweetheart.
*The girl's man started taking care of his sweetheart.*

Vúra kumakâarim kích.
Just sort-of-bad only.
*She kept only getting worse.*

## ARUTÂANAHITIHIRAK

Xás pamu'áka káru pamútaat kunpíip, "Chími yúruk êem píkan!"
Then her-father and her-mother they-told-him, "Downriver doctor go-summon!"
*Then her father and mother told the young man to go summon a particular doctor from downriver.*

Xás uvâaram.
Then he-went.
*So, he went.*

Kunipêer, "Vaa káan i'áhoovish Iknûumin. Vaa uum ûumukich."
They-told him, "That there you-will-be-walking Iknûumin. That it-is close."
*They had told him he must take the Iknûumin Mountain trail. It is the closest way.*

Xás vaa u'áhoo.
So that he-went.
*So, that's the way he went.*

Firipámyuusa xás ukvíripish.
Firipámyuusa-village then he-started-to-run.
*When he approached Firipámyuusa he started to run.*

Káan xás pa'êem umah.
There the-doctor he-found.
*He found the doctor there.*

## ARARAPÍKVA

Xás upêer, "Chôora, nupíkarukti. Nanikeechíkyav tookúha."
Then he-told-her, "Let's-go, I-have-come-to-fetch-you. My-sweetheart she-is-sick."
*Then he told the doctor, "I have come to bring you back with me. My sweetheart is sick. Let's go."*

Ta'ítam uvâaramaheen.
So she-went.
*So, the doctor left with him.*

Xás upiip, "Naa vúra áavkam tani'ípahoo."
Then he-said, "I just in-front I-am-travelling-on."
*The man told the doctor that he was going to travel on ahead of her.*

Kúkuum vaa vúra káan u'ípahoo Iknûumin.
Again that just there he-travelled Iknûumin.
*He travelled back along the Iknûumin Mountain trail again.*

Vari máruk chími upikfúkuvraavish, axmáy vúra hûutva u'iin.
Towards uphill he-was-just-about-to-crest-over, suddenly just he-felt-odd.
*As he was about to crest over the mountain ridge, he suddenly began feeling strange.*

"Manâa kanikyívish." Kárumaník uxúti, "Íshki kan'áhoo."
"It-seems I-am-going-to-fall." The-fact-is he-is-thinking, "Fast I-want-to-go."
*(He said to himself) "It seems like I'm going to fall down." Actually he was thinking, "I'll walk faster!"*

## ARUTÂANAHITIHIRAK

Xás uxús, "Naa nixúti tu'iv pananikeechíkyav."
Then he-thought, "I I-am-thinking already-she-is-dead my-sweetheart."
*And, then intuitively he thought his sweetheart had just died. (Hence his strange feelings.)*

Ii, xás pakáruk utrôovuti poopikfúkuvraa.
Ooh, then upriver he-looked-upriverwards when-he-crested-over.
*He had a lonesome feeling as he crested the ridge and looked north.*

Axmáy káruk fáatva umah.
Suddenly upriver something he-saw.
*Then he saw something startling in the north!*

Xás uhyárihish, xás uxús, "Káruma vaa nanikeechíkyav patánimah."
He-stood-still, then he-thought, "The-fact-is, that my-sweetheart that-I-am-seeing."
*He stood still, and thought that what he was seeing was his sweetheart.*

Chavúra ta ûumukich.
Finally, already close-by.
*Whatever it was, it was now very close.*

Uxús, "Vúra ni'axaychákishriheesh."
He-thought, "Just I-am-going-to-grab-her."
*And he thought it was close enough that he could grab the apparition.*

Póomahti.
He-looked-at-it.
*He looked at her.*

Ararávaas u'ásati, axváak u'íshipva pamunhíkar vúra.
Indian-blanket she-was-wearing, on-her-head it-was-tied her-drawstring just.
*She was wearing a buckskin blanket that was tied to her head by a leather tie-string.*

Vari yiimúsich vúra ukxiptánmaahti pamúvaas.
Towards little-ways just it-floats-without-any-reason her-blanket.
*The deerskin blanket was floating out and away from her head for no apparent reason.*

Xás u'axaychákish. Purafâat vúra áfishara.
Then he-grabbed-her. Nothing just he-touched.
*Then he grabbed for her, but he felt only air.*

Peekréemyah kích kúnish úkuuyvuti.
The-wind just sort-of it-blew-on-him.
*He only felt a wind blow on him as she passed by.*

Xás yûum xás umah, xás u'áharam.
Then a-little-ways-south he-saw-her, then he-followed.
*Then he saw her just below him, and he started to follow her.*

Xás tá yiimúsich káan úkraam u'íithra.
Then already a-little-ways there lake it-stands.
*He followed her for a short distance, to where a lake stood.*

Axmáy vaa ukvíripath.
Suddenly that she-runs-around.
*Suddenly she started running around the lake.*

Ífuth vúra, chavúra itaharâan upikviripiróopiithva.
Behind just, finally ten times she-ran-around.
*He was following behind, and finally, she ran around the lake ten times.*

Xás úskaakuri.
Then she-jumped-into-the-water.
*Then she jumped into the lake.*

Ífuth vúra, ivaxráhak xás úskaakish pa'ávansa.
Behind just, a-dried-up-place then he-jumped the man.
*He was behind her, and when he jumped into the lake, it was dried up.*

Xás kúkuum vúra itaharâan upikvíripath.
Then again just ten-times he-ran-around.
*Then he ran around the lake ten times again.*

Xás úskaakuri.
Then he-jumped-into-water.
*Then he jumped into the waters of the lake.*

Yánava ímpáah u'íshipva.
He-saw trail it-is-starting-out.
*(When he came out of the water) he looked around and saw a trail head.*

Xás ukvíripuni.
Then he-ran-down.
*Then, he went running down the trail.*

Vúra vaa tu'áhooheen.
Just that-way she-had-walked.
*His sweetheart had gone that way.*

Vúraník umáhmaahti.
Just he-caught-a-glimpse-of-her.
*(As he followed) he kept catching glimpses of her ahead.*

Chavúra tá yiiv.
Finally already long-ways.
*Finally, they had gone a long ways.*

Axmáy vúra uthítiv poo'ákakurihti.
Suddenly just he-heard that-they-were-hollering.
*And, suddenly he heard people hollering.*

Imtananáamnihich vúra pakunipíti.
Very-discernible just what-they-were-saying.
*Their words were very clear.*

"Ípihara xáy ôok!"
"Bones-having don't here."
*"Anyone with bones mustn't be here!"*

Xás uxus, "Naa pakanéepeenti."
Then he-thought, "I they-are-talking-to-me."
*He knew he was the one they were talking to.*

Káruma vúra tu'ûumukich.
The-fact-is just already-it-is-close-by.
*The hollering came close-by.*

Chími kunithvíripishriheesh.
They-were-about-to-start-out-running.
*The man and woman started running down. (He was still following her.)*

Yánava káan kêech vúra pa'ipuunváramhiti.
He-saw there big just where-it-is-a-resting-place.
*He saw a very big resting place there.*

Ishvírip u'íihya.
Pine-tree it-is-standing.
*A pine tree stood there.*

Yánava axmáy káan úpshaamkir pamúvaas.
He-saw suddenly there she-left-behind her-blanket.
*And he saw her suddenly leave her deerskin blanket there at the tree.*

Á' upáthtak.
Up she-threw-it.
*She threw the blanket up in the air.*

Vári pooturáayva, pa'ípaha âapun kúnish tu'êevish,
Towards that-he-looked-around, the-tree on-the-ground sort-of it-bent-downwards,
*As he looked about he saw that the tree was bent over nearly to the ground,*

## ARARAPÍKVA

pávaas pakáan kunípshaamkirihti, pakóo kunfíiphiti.
the-blanket that-there they-had-left-behind, the-all they-died-off.
*from the weight of the deerskin blankets left behind by all those who had died before.*

Xás kunithvíripuni.
Then they-ran-down.
*Then they ran on down the path.*

Vaa kích poo'ákakurihti,
That only that-they-were-hollering-to-him,
*The other voices were hollering the whole time,*

"Ípihara tá ôok.
"Bones-having already here.
*"A person with bones is here.*

Xáy ôok!"
Don't here!"
*Leave here!"*

Astíip kunithvíripish.
River's-edge they-ran-to-it.
*The girl ran down to the river's edge.*

Ta'ítam kunvítivrikaheen.
So, they-rowed-over-to-meet-someone.
*Some people rowed across the river in a canoe to meet her.*

Ma'vánihich uhyárihish pa'ávansa.
A-little-ways-uphill he-stood the-man.
*The man stopped a little ways uphill.*

Úmuusti pamukeechíkyav.
He-looked-at his-sweetheart.
*He watched his sweetheart.*

Ithyáruk tá kunvíitkara.
Across-the-river already they-rowed-across-water.
*They rowed her across the river.*

Xás mâam upárihraa, pa'ávansa.
Then uphill he-walked-back-uphill, the-man.
*Then the man went back up the hill.*

Káan xás ukrîish.
There then he-sat.
*He sat there.*

Vaa kích kun'ákakurihti,
That only they-were-hollering,
*The other voices were hollering all this time,*

"Ípihara xáy ôok!"
"Bones-having don't here!"
*"Ones with bones mustn't be here."*


Umuustíhvunaati.
He-was-looking-at-them.
*And, then the man watched some other people.*

Peethyáa ukúrini.
Fish-dam they-were-sitting.
*They were sitting on a fish dam.*

# ARARAPÍKVA

Vaa káan pakun'irukûuntakoo,
That there that-they-were-sitting-on,
*The people he was watching were sitting there,*

    pa'áraaras pakunikríihvuti.
    the-people that-they-were-fishing.
    *and fishing.*

Chavúra ukxáramha.
Finally it-got-dark.
*Finally, it got dark.*

Xás sâam astíip kúuk u'uum.
Then downhill at-river's-edge there he-arrived.
*Then the man went down to the shore of the river.*

Vari ithyáruk poothítiimkarati yithumásva poothívishhiti.
Towards across-the-river he-heard-across-the-water different-kinds they-were-celebrating.
*Across the river he could hear them celebrating with different kinds of dances.*

Xás vaa káan astíip úkrii.
Then that there river's-edge he-sat.
*The man just sat there at the river's edge.*

Vári patusúpaa kári mâam tóopnaa.
Towards it's-day still uphill already-he-went-uphill.
*About daybreak he went back up the hill.*

Mâam xás tupikrîish.
Uphill then again-he-sat.
*When he got uphill, he sat down.*

# ARUTÂANAHITIHIRAK

Sáruk tupitfákuti.
Downhill he-looked-down-from-uphill.
*He looked down the hill.*

Kúkuum vúra patookxúrar kári kúuk astíip, kúuk tu'íipma.
Again just when-it-got-dark still there-to river's-edge, there-to he-returned.
*When it got dark again he went back down to the riverbank.*

Káan úkrii.
There he-sat.
*He sat there.*

Uthítiimti pakunchúuphiti, pakunikríihvunaati
He-heard as-they-were-talking, as they-were-fishing
*He heard people talking, as they fished*

>peethyáahak.
>the-fish-dam-at.
>*at the fish dam.*

Chavúra itroopatishamnihéekxaram.
Finally nine-nights.
*Finally nine nights came and passed.*

Astíip uvíishriv.
River's-edge he-kept-returning.
*He kept going down to the water's edge.*

Pu'ávara fâatva.
Did-not-eat something.
*The man hadn't eaten a thing.*

Kích uxúti,
Only he-thinks,
*All he thought was,*

> "Ník uum vúra hûut nikupa'íipmaheesh pámita ni'aramsîiprivirak?"
> "Seems it's just how I-am-sort-of-going-to-return where-formerly I-started-out?"
> *"I wonder how I'm going to get back to where I came from."*

Xás vaa káan kustúrivak ukûuntakoo.
Then that there river-grass-on he-sat-down.
*He sat on a tuft of grass that grew along the river.*

Axmáy uthítiv yûum, súva kunchúuphiti.
Suddenly he-heard a-little-ways-downriverwards, he-heard they-were-talking.
*Suddenly he heard people talking a little ways downstream from where he was sitting.*

Xás uxus, "Akáray áta, kíri nichuphûunish."
Then he-thought, "Who I-wonder, let-it-be I-am-talking-to-them."
*And he thought, "I wonder who it is, I want to talk with them."*

Chavúra tá ûumukich, súva yítha upíti,
Finally already close-by, he-heard one he-said,
*They got close to him and he heard one of them say,*

> "Hôoy payêem nu'êereesh?"
> "Where now we-are-going-to-fish?"
> *"Where shall we go to fish now?"*

Xás yítha upiip,
Then one he-said,
*Then one of them said,*

"Xâatik Xumkáak musâam nu'êeri."
"May-it-be Xumkáak-village its-downill we-are-fishing."
*"Let's fish below Xumkáak village."*

"Chémi."
"All right."
*"All right."*

Xás pakáan ikréen uxús,
Then the-there one-who-was-sitting he-thought,
*The one who was sitting there, the man, thought,*

"Hôoy áta káru vaa úthvuuyti?
"Where I-wonder and that-it-is-named?
*"I wonder where that place they named is?*

Káruma pani'aramsîiprivtiheerak vaa úthvuuy."
The-fact-is where-I-come-from-place that it-is-called."
*The fact is, the place where I come from has the same name."*

Chavúra mupîimach takunvíitraa.
Finally his-beside they-rowed-up-from-downstream.
*Finally they rowed right up beside him.*

Xás upíip, "Akáray iimkun? Matêe, kanachuphûunishhi."
Then he-said, "Who you-folks? Wait-a-moment, speak-to-me."
*The man asked, "Who are you folks? Wait a moment! Speak to me."*

Xás kunishkáxish káan.
Then they-stopped there.
*Then, the people stopped there to talk to him.*

Xás kunipêer, "Iim úm míta kunípaat Ípihara tu'áhoo?"
Then they-said-to-him, "You? former they-said Bones-having he-has-come?"
*They asked him, "Are you the one they were telling us about earlier? The one with bones?"*

Xás upiip, "Hãa, naa vaa."
Then he-said, "Yes, I that."
*He said, "Yes, I'm that one."*

[The fishermen then told the man that his sweetheart was in Indian Heaven.]

Xás kunipêer, "Imáan xasík îikam uvôonupukeesh pamikeechíkyav.
Then they-said, "Tomorrow it-will-be outside she-is-going-to-go-outdoors your-sweetheart.
*Then they told him, "Tomorrow your sweetheart will be going outdoors (for the first time since arriving).*

Payêem úum kári mu'ípih kunpikyâati.
Now she still her-bones they-are-fixing.
*Right now they are still removing her bones (in preparation for her life in heaven).*

## ARUTÂANAHITIHIRAK

Váa kúth peethyáruk táay u'íthívishhiti."
That because-of that-across-river lots it-is-singing-and-ceremonial-dancing."
*That's the reason for all the dancing and singing across the river."*

"Kíri nipchuphûunishhi, xasík nipvâarameesh."
"May-it-be I-am-talking-to-her, let-it-be I-am-going-back-home."
*The man told them, "I want to talk with her again. I am going to go back home."*

Xás kunipêer, "Nuu vúra payêem numúsareesh."
Then they-told-him, "We just now we-are-going-to-go-see-her."
*They told him they were going to go see her right then.*

Peexútihaak "Kiri vaa uthítiiv pa'íim ôok."
When-you-are-thinking "May-it-be that she-hears that-you-here."
*And they told the man, "If you were thinking, 'I hope she hears that I am here in the Indian Heaven'"*

[We will tell her that you are here.]

Xás upiip, "Fâat chími kiik'ásaanveeshap?
Then he-says, "What I-am-going-to-offer-in-payment-to-you-folks?
*Then he asked them what they wanted in payment to take his message across to his sweetheart.*

Nani'úhraam vaa vúra kích ni'êethti, káru nanithántut."
My-pipe that just alone I-am-packing, and my black-paint."
*"All I've brought with me is my pipe and my black paint."*

Xás kunpiip, "Vaa vúra kin'ásanvi."
Then they-said, "That just you-offer-us-in-payment."
*And, they said, "Offer us that then."*

Xás upiip, "Chémi."
Then he-said, "All right."
*"All right," he said.*

Xás kunipêer, "Tanumúsara pamikeechíkyav.
Then they-said, "We-are-going-to-go-see your-sweetheart.
*"We are going to go see your sweetheart now," they told him.*

Hûut nupêereesh?"
How we-shall-say-to-her?"
*"What shall we say to her?"*

Xás upiip, "Kupêesh ik, ôok níkrii. Vári tá nithákaariha vúra."
Then he-said, "You-folks-shall-tell-her must, here I-am. Towards by-now I-am-perishing just."
*He said, "You folks tell her that I'm here. Tell her that I'm nearly starved to death."*

Xás kuniyâaram, ithyáruk kunvítish. Xás máruk kun'ínaa.
Then they-went, across-the-river they-landed-a-canoe.
Then uphill they-went.
*They left the man and landed their redwood canoe across the river. Then they walked up the hill.*

Chavúra kuma'îikam kun'uum pakáan ukrêerak.
Finally its-outside they-arrived where-there she-is.
*Finally they arrived just outside the house there where the man's sweetheart was staying.*

Iinâak kunthítiimfurukti yithumásva uthívishhiti.
Inside they-heard-indoors different-kinds ceremonial-singing-and-dancing.
*Inside the house they heard all kinds of different ceremonial dancing and singing.*

Chavúra iinâakukam kun'uum.
Finally inside they-went.
*Finally they went into the house.*

Kun'áathvuti. Puráan kunípeenti, "Íim chuphûunishhi."
They-were-afraid. One-to-the-other they-were-telling, "You talk-to-her."
*The men were afraid. They told each other, "You talk to her."*

Xás yítha'îin kunchuphûunish.
Then one-by he-talked-to-her.
*Then one of them spoke to her.*

Úyruuhriv.
She-was-lying-down.
*She was lying down.*

Xás upêer, "Ithyáruk pamikeechíkyav úkrii.
Then he-told-her, "Across-the-river your-sweetheart he-is.
*Then he told her, "Your sweetheart is across the river.*

Vári ixuséentihap 'kiri nipchuphûunish.
Towards he-is-thinking, 'May-it-be I-want I-am-talking-to-her.
*He is thinking about you and wants to talk with you.*

Xasík nipvâarameesh.'
It-will-be I-return-am-going-to-go.'
*He said he is going back home.*

Nuu nupípasipreevish."
We we-will-take-him."
*We will be taking him back home."*

Xás upiip, "Kêemachkoo, íf xára ôok tóokrii. Fâat u'áamti?"
Then she-said, "Poor-thing, truly long-time here he-has-been. What he-is-eating?"
*She said, "Oh, my poor darling! He's been here for so long! What has he been eating?"*

Xás kunpiip, "Uhêerati, vaa vúra kich."
Then they-said, "He-is-smoking, that-is-all."
*They told her, "All he does is smoke his pipe (he hasn't eaten)."*

Xás upiip, "Vúraník vaa nixúti, hûut tukupavúraayvaha.
Then she-said, "Just that I-am-thinking, how he-is-sort-of-going-around.
*She told them, "I was wondering about that, how he's able to get around.*

Yakún ni'áapunmuti ôok mít u'áhoot.
You-see I-know here formerly he-came.
*You see, I knew that he came here.*

Vári chími kiikpêerana imáan kuméekxaram
Towards you-folks-tell-him tomorrow its-night
*You folks tell him that tomorrow night*

xasík nichuphûunisheesh."
going-to-be I-am-going-to-talk-to-him."
*I will talk to him."*

Xás kunpiyâaram, ithyáruk kunipvítish.
Then they-went-back, across-the-river they-landed-again.
*The men went back to where the man was waiting. They landed the boat again across the river.*

Xás kunipêer, "Imáan kuméekxaram xasík ichuphûunisheeshap."
Then they-said, "Tomorrow it's-night-time going-to-be she-is-going-to-talk-to-you."
*They told the man that his sweetheart said she would talk to him the following night.*

# ARARAPÍKVA

Xás mâam kúuk u'íipma.
Then uphill to-there he-went-back.
*He went back up the hill after talking with them.*

Pasúpaaha kích uxúti, "Púya chími ukxáramha.
As-the-day-broke only he-thought, "May-it-be it-is-dark.
*At daybreak all he thought was, "I wish it was already dark.*

> Xás nichuphûunish nanikeechíkyav."
> Then I-talk my-sweetheart."
> *Because then I would be talking with my sweetheart."*

Xás pookxáramha, astíip kúuk u'íipma.
Then when-it-got-dark, river's-edge there he-returned.
*When it got dark he went down to the river's edge.*

Axmáy kunchúupha. Súva tá kunvíitraa.
Suddenly they-were-talking. He-heard they-were-paddling-downstream.
*Suddenly he heard them talking. He heard them paddling down the river.*

Xás káan kunishkáxish.
Then there they-stopped.
*And they stopped there where he was.*

Xás kunipêer, "Chéemyaach váramnihi páahak!"
Then they-told-him, "Hurry up, jump-in the-canoe-in!"
*They told him, "Quick! Jump into the canoe!"*

Xás uváramni.
Then he-jumped-in.
*Then he jumped into the canoe.*

## ARUTÂANAHITIHIRAK

Ithyáruk kunvítish, tá ára kunvítish.
Across-the-river they-beached-the canoe, already person they-landed-the-canoe.
*They landed the canoe across the river. The man was across the river.*

Xás kunipêer, "Ôok vúra íkrii páahak."
Then they-told-him, "Here just you-stay canoe-in."
*They told him to stay in the canoe.*

Xás máruk kun'ínaa.
Then uphill they-went.
*Then they went up the hill.*

Xás kunipêer, "Sâam páahak mikeechíkyav."
Then they-told-her, "Downhill canoe-in your-sweetheart."
*They told the girl, "Your sweetheart is in the canoe down at the river."*

Kunipêer, "Vaa kári upvâarameesh peechuphûunishhaak."
They-told-her, "That still he-is-going-to-go-back-home when-you-talk-to-him."
*They told her that he was still going to go back home after talking to her.*

Xás upiip, "Naa káru vúra nipvâarameesh."
Then she-said, "That also just I-am-going-back-home."
*Then she told the men, "I am going to go back with him."*

Xás upiip, "Naa káru vúra tanipvâaram."
Then she-said, "I also just I-am-going-back-home."
*She said that she was going to return home, too.*

85

## ARARAPÍKVA

Xás kunipêer, "Chéemyaach, manâa xáy kun'áapunma pa'áraar."
Then they-told-her, "Hurry-up, let-it-be don't they-know the-people."
*Then they told her, "Hurry up then, the other people mustn't know what you are going to do."*

Xás sáruk kunpávyiihma páahak.
Then downhill they-back-went-down boat-at.
*Then they went back downhill to the canoe.*

Xás kunipêer, "Âapun kiikíxupish."
Then they-said, "Down you-folks-lay-on-your-chest-side."
*The oarsmen told the lovers to lay face down in the canoe.*

Xás váas kinpathxútap.
Then deerskin-blanket they-covered-them.
*Then they covered the lovers with a deerskin blanket.*

"Xáy kutúraayva. Kiik'íchunvuti."
"Don't you-two-look-around. You-folks-hide."
*They told them, "Don't look around. Keep yourselves hidden."*

Xás kunípvitshur.
Then they-paddled-off.
*Then they set off.*

Xás vaa kunkupa'áapunmahiti, káruk paah tá kunipvítroov.
Then thus they-sort-of-knew, upriver canoe already they-back-paddling.
*The lovers sensed that the canoe was moving upstream.*

## ARUTÂANAHITIHIRAK

Chavúra tá yiiv.
Finally already long-ways.
*Finally, they had travelled a long ways.*

Xás kunvítish.
Then they-beached-the-canoe.
*Then they landed on shore.*

Xás pa'ávansa kunipêer,
Then the-man they-told-him,
*Then they told the man,*

    "Chéemyaach máruk pikvíripraa; pípan tanu'ípak."
    "Hurry-up, uphill run-uphill; say we-have-come-back."
    *"Hurry now! Run uphill to the village and tell everyone that you two have come back!"*

Xás upikvíripraa.
Then he-ran-uphill.
*Then, he went running up the hill.*

Xás upiip, "tanu'ípak."
Then he-said, "We-came-back."
*Then he told the people, "We have come back."*

Xás koovúra kuníxrar.
Then all-of-them they-cried.
*Then all the villagers cried.*

Xás upiip, "Xáyfaat kúxrar.
Then he-said, "Don't you-folks-cry.
*He told them not to cry.*

◢‖ 87 ‖◣

## ARARAPÍKVA

Chéemyaach kiikpiktíiti paaxvithíni piríshriik.
Hurry-up, you-folks-tear-it-up the-grave trees-among.
*They should hurry and take apart his young sweetheart's grave in the woods.*

Kiipsharíshriihvi pakukyávanik."
You-folks-carry-it-back what-you-folks-did-long-ago."
*"Return all the dirt that you moved from the gravesite."*

Xás kunipsharíshriihva.
Then they-carried-it-back.
*So, the villagers packed all the dirt out.*

Xás sáruk upikvíripuni.
Then downhill he-back-ran-down.
*Then the man ran back down the hill to the canoe.*

Xás kunpiip,
Then they-said,
*Then the man was told by the oarsmen,*

"Itaharasúpaahak, xasík îim uvôonupukeesh.
"Ten-days-at, let-it-be outside she-is-going-to-go-outdoors.
*"Your sweetheart can go outdoors after ten days.*

Mâaka sivrihvamâam véek káan ukrêevish."
In-the-back uphill-wall-side-of-house that-must there she-is-going-to-stay."
*She must remain secluded in the far back corner of the living house, the mâaka sivrihvamâam."*

Xás kunipêer pa'ávansa,
Then they-told-him the man,
*Then they told the man,*

"Íim káru vúra véek kóo. Xasík arará'îin kiikmáheeshap.
"You also just that-must all. Going-to-be people-by you-folks-going-to-be-seen-by-them.
*"You must stay secluded, too. Only then can you be seen by other people.*

Kíshvuuf kích kupáatvutiheesh.
Angelica-root only you-two-going-to-bathe-with.
*You two must bathe using the kíshvuuf (angelica) root in water.*

Vaa mûuk ikpíhan kupipmahóonkooneesh."
That by-means-of strong you-two-will-feel."
*Using the angelica root will make you both regain your strength to live again."*

Xás máruk kunpínaa.
Then uphill they-back-went.
*Then the two sweethearts went uphill.*

Káru uumkun tá kunipvíitshur.
And they they-paddled-off.
*And the oarsmen paddled off.*

Xás máruk iinâak sivrihvamâam káan kun'iin.
Then uphill indoors uphill-side-of-house-in-back there they-stayed.
*Then they stayed inside in the back of the house.*

Vúra pukinmáahtihap.
Just not-they-were-seen-by-them.
*None of the villagers saw them during their seclusion.*

Kíshvuuf kích kunpáatvuti.
Angelica-root only you-two-going-to-bathe-with.
*They bathed using only the angelica root as they had been told.*

Teetaharasúpaa xás kun'iruvôonupuk.
Already-ten-days then they-came-outdoors.
*Ten days passed and then the lovers came out of their house, out of their seclusion.*

Vári koovúra xúus kuniptárari pakínmah. Kúnish tákin'ay.
Towards all they-were-surprised that-they-saw-them. Sort-of they-were-afraid-of-them.
*Everyone was surprised to see the sweethearts. The villagers were a little afraid of them.*

Chavúra tá xára. Axíich tá kunthíinati. Vúra yâamach kunkupa'íinahiti.
Finally already long-time. Child by-now they-had. Just nice they-sort-of-lived.
*Finally they had been back in the village for a long time. They had a child. The sweethearts lived a very nice life.*

Chavúra tá kêech pamukún'arama.
Finally already big their-child.
*Their boy was getting big.*

Vári îikam paaxichríik úxtiivhiti.
Towards outdoors the-children-among he-played.
*He was always playing with the children outside.*

Axmáyik takunipêer,
Suddenly-at-one-time already-they-told-him,
*Suddenly one time, the other children told the boy,*

> "Ník áta puyâahara'ípakara itáathiti."
> "Yet perhaps dead-person-come-back your-mother-is."
> *"Your mother came back from the dead."*

Xás pamu'áka îin takunipêer, "Xáyfaat mítaat i'éethi."
Then his-father by he-told-him, "Don't your-mother you-tell-her."
*When the boy told his father what the other children said to him, his father told him never to tell his mother what the children said to him.*

Iinâak toopvôonfuruk paaxiich.
Indoors already-he-again-goes-indoors the-child.
*The boy went into the house.*

Xás mútaat îin takunipêer, "Hûut ípeentihap?"
Then his-mother she-said-to-him, "How they-say-to-you?"
*Then his mother asked him, "What do the children say to you?"*

Xás toopiip, "Púrahuun."
Then he-said, "Nothing-harmful."
*And the boy told her, "Nothing much."*

Chavúra tá pâanpay kêech sípnuuk uvíikti.
Finally already after-awhile large round-storage-basket she-is-weaving.
*After some time passed the mother was weaving a large round storage basket.*

Axmáy îim úxrar pamú'arama.
Suddenly outdoors he-was-crying her-child.
*Suddenly, she heard her boy crying outdoors.*

Xás upvôonfuruk.
Then he-came-indoors.
*And he came running inside the house.*

Xás upêer, "Hûut ti'iin?"
Then she-told-him, "How you-are?"
*She asked, "What's the matter with you?"*

Xás upiip, "Kaneeykárati. Kanéepeenti,
Then he-said, "They-beat-me-up. They-told-me,
*And the boy told her, "They beat me up. They told me,*

> 'Ník áta puyâahara'ípakara itáathiti.'"
> 'Yet perhaps dead-person-having-returned your-mother-being.'"
> *'Your mother is a dead person who came back.'"*

# ARUTÂANAHITIHIRAK

Xás upiip, "Chémi, kanipvâarami."
Then she-said, "All right, I-am-going-back-home."
*She said, "All right, I am going to leave."*

Xás pamuvíikar koovúra yíchaach upíkyav.
Then her-weaving-materials all-of-them together she-fixed.
*She gathered together all of her weaving materials.*

Pamuvíkapu upmáhyaan.
Her-woven-carrying-basket she-put-in.
*She put the materials into her carrying basket.*

Xás áhkaam úkyav.
Then fire-big she-made.
*Then she made a big fire.*

Xás vaa káan áak u'íithkiri pamuvíkaha.
Then that there fire-in she-put-it-into-fire her-weaving.
*Then she put the basket she was weaving into the fire.*

Xás úskaakramni.
Then she-jumped-into.
*Then she jumped into the basket.*

Táma vúra upvôonfuruk pa'ávansa.
Then just he-went-indoors the-man.
*At that moment the father came into the house.*

[He knew what had just happened.]

## ARARAPÍKVA

Xás upêer pamú'arama,
Then he-told his-child,
*Then he told his boy,*

> "Atafâat ti'éethi pamítaat paaxîich îin ípeentihap."
> "Perhaps you-told your-mother the-children-by they-told-you."
> *"Maybe you told your mother what the other kids were saying to you."*

Xás upiip, "Hãa."
Then he-said, "Yes."
*The boy said, "Yes."*

Xás kunipêer, "Vaa kumá'ii toopvâaram pamítaat."
Then he-told-the-boy, "That because-of she-went-back your-mother."
*Then he told the boy, "That's the reason why your mother returned to that place."*

Xás póomuusti. Axmáy Yumaaraxatímniim
Then he-looked-at-her. Suddenly dead-man's-butterfly
*Then the man looked. Suddenly a giant spirit-moth*

> úkxiiprupuk chancháaksurak.
> it-flew-through smokehole-at.
> *flew out through the smokehole in the roof of the living house.*

Máh vúrava pumáahtihap.
Seeing whatever they-were-not-seeing.
*He just saw it before it disappeared.*

P úyava mupâapuhanik.
Behold her-words-in-ancient-times.
*And here are the woman's last words.*

"Yáas'ára. Xâat fâatva kumayíkiha. Kíshvuuf upáat-
vutiheesh,
"Human Being. Even-if whatever its-sickness. Angelica-
root he-will-bathe,
*"Human Beings! It doesn't matter what kind of sickness it is.*
*You must bathe using the angelica root,*

    váa ánavheesh, paxúnutich upmahóonkoonatihaak."
    that medicine-going-to-be, when-thin he-is-feeling."
    *that's your best medicine, when you feel weak."*

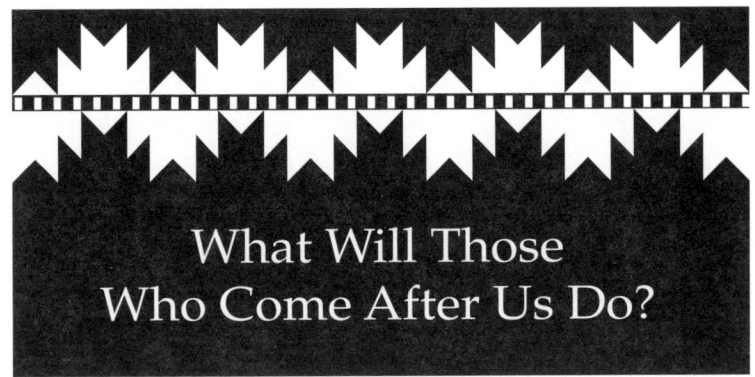

# What Will Those Who Come After Us Do?

In this recording of elders from the first quarter of this century, we find a bittersweet consideration of the future of the Karuk People and the Karuk belief system. Their words evoke the ideal Karuk world, a world that is distinctly spiritual and defined by the presence of divinity in all things. Yet so much has been forgotten, so much is slipping away: this has been a terrible problem for Karuk people ever since the coming of whitemen.

Today the elders still remind us that if we follow the ways of the old people, and the Ikxaréeyavs, we cannot go wrong. In this story, the elders ask the haunting question: What will happen if we forget those ordained and divine ways? This story is a reminder to all of us that the Karuk way and, in fact, the ways of all the indigenous peoples, must be protected. The story also points out that *we* are the responsible ones. This is *our* time, and *our* place.

## ARARAPÍKVA

Vaa vúra kích pakunmáharatihanik Peekxaréeyavsa.
That just only that-they-followed-long-ago the Spirit-People.
*The Old People were following the Ikxaréeyavs, the Spirit People, all the time.*

Koovúra vaa kunkupítihanik; pahûut Peekxaréyav kunkupítihanik, vaa kunkupíti.
All that they-did-long-ago, the-how the-Spirit-People they-did-in-ancient-times, that-they-did.
*All the People did the same long ago; whatever the Spirit People did, the People did.*

Xás pávaa pakun'áamtihanik Peekxaréeyav, víri vaa kích pakun'áamti.
So, the-that they-ate-in-ancient-times the-Spirit-People, so that only that-they-ate.
*And the things that the Ikxaréeyavs ate, that was all that the Old People ate.*

Vaa kinípeeranik, "Véek páy ku'áamtiheesh.
That they-told-them-long-ago, "That-must this you-folks-going-to-be-eating.
*That's what they were told, "You must eat this kind of food.*

    Peekxaréeyav áama kun'áamtihanik, xuun kunpátatihanik, áama xákaan xuun.
    The-Spirit-People salmon they-were-eating-in-ancient-times, acorn-soup they-spooned-up, salmon together acorn-soup.
    *The Ikxaréeyavs ate salmon and they spooned up acorn soup, eating salmon along with acorn soup.*

Káru pufích'iish kun'áamtihanik."
And deer-meat they-ate-anciently."
*And they ate deermeat."*

Vaa vúra pakunfúhishtihanik, Peekxaréeyav axakyâanich vúra kun'ípamtihanik,
That just that-they-believed-long-ago, the Spirit People only-two-times just they-ate-in-ancient-times,
*And the Old People claimed that the Ikxaréeyavs ate two meals a day,*

vaa vúra kích pakunkupítihanik.
that just only that-they-did-long-ago.
*and so that's the way the Old People did as well.*

Pa'apxantínihich pakunivyíhukanik, xás vaa kunípaanik, "Kêemish pakun'áamti,
When-the-little-wide-hats they-came, then that they-said, "Poison that-they-are-eating,
*When the white people all came, the Old People said that they were eating food poisonous to Indians.*

kemisha'ávaha, ithivthaneentaniha'ávaha."
poison-food, earth-coming-to-an-end-food."
*It was poison food, world-come-to-an-end food.*

Achíphan vúra va'áraaras vaa kích papishîich kun'ávanik pa'apxantiich'ávaha.
Middle-one just its-people that only the-first they-ate the-little-wide-hat's-food.
*The middle aged people were the first to eat the white man's food.*

Víri pakunvíshtar, vúra kunvíshtar. Puráan kunipêer, "Vúra uum amáyav."
So when-they-liked-to-eat-it, just they-liked-to-eat-it. To-each-other they-told, "Just it good-tasting-food."
*When they liked it, they really liked it. Then they told each other, "It's good tasting food."*

Xás tákunpiip, "Ník'áta vúra uum pu'íimtihara. Naa táni'av, pasára."
Then they-said, "Yet-perhaps just he-did-not-die. I I-ate, the-bread."
*They said, "He never died. I am going to eat it, that white man's bread."*

Xás vaa koovúra papihnîichas káru pakéevniikichas xára xás kun'ávanik.
Then that all-of-them the-old-men and-the-old-women long-time then they-ate-it.
*It was a long time before the Old Men and Old Women ate the white man's food.*

Nuu ta'ifuchtîimichas pávaa nu'áapunmuti
We already-the-last-ones that-that we-know
*We are the last ones that know*

> pávaa Peekxaréeyav pakunkupítihanik; vaa kun-áamtihaak.
> the-that the-Spirit-People that-they-did; that they-ate.
> *how the Ikxaréeyavs used to do, all that they used to eat.*

## ARARÁCHUUPHA

Pámitva kinípeentihat pananutaat îin.
What-previously they-told-us our-mother by.
*Our mothers told us that.*

Víri vaa vúra nuu káru vaa tapukin'áamtihara,
So that just we too that we-are-not-eating,
*And even we do not eat any more,*

    pámitva kinípeerat, "Veek ku'áamtiheesh."
    what-formerly they-told-us, "That-must you-folks-going-to-be-eating."
    *what they told us before, "You must eat this kind."*

Hûutheesh pananu'ífuth va'ífapuhsa?
How-it-will-be the-behind-us its-being-raised-up-ones?
*And what will they who are raised after us do?*

# Glossary

## a

'á', *up.*
áachip, *middle, center.*
áah, *fire.*
áama, *salmon.*
âapun, *on the ground.*
áapunma, *to know (a fact), to know about (a person or thing), to find out.*
áathva, *to be afraid.*
áavkam, *in front, ahead; "face-side."*
-ach, *diminutive.*
áfish, *to touch, to feel (with hands).*
Afrîich, *personal name. No mg.*
áharam, *to follow.*
áhoo, *to travel, to walk.*
ahóokiri, *to walk on, by way of.*
-ak, *on, in, by.*
áka, *father.*
ákakuri, *(pl.) to shout.*
akáray, akâay, *who? anyone.*
akraa, *(lamprey) eel.*
amáyav, *good tasting.*
Ameekyáaraam, *placename. Mg. "where-they-fix-the-salmon."*
ánav, *medicine.*
anoo, *ouch! Also, anôo.*
ánxuut, *headdress, "hanger."*
ápsuun, *snake.*
apxantínihich, *white man: "little-flat-cap." Also,* apxantîich.
ára, *person.*
áraara, *person, man (human being); Indian.*
áraarahiti, *(pl.) to live.*
-arama, *child (offspring)*
aramsîip(riv), *to start out (on a journey); to come from (a certain place).*
arara'íhvunaa, *Brush Dance. Mg. "people-dancing."*
aráriik, *village, town, city. Means "people-place."*
árih-, *to jump, move quickly; to go.*
árihishish(ri), *to become, to be transformed into.*
as, *stone, rock.*
ása, *to wear (on one's body).*
ásaanva, *to offer payment.*
asiktávaan, *woman.*
astiip, *on the river bank.*
áta, *perhaps, I wonder.*
atafâat, *perhaps, maybe.*
ataháriva, *at one time.*
ataychúkinach, *special word for Indian potatoes, brodiaea (táyiith). Mg. "little-blue-salmon-eggs."*
Á'uuyich, *placename. Sugar Loaf Mountain. Mg. "little-above-mountain."*
av, *to eat.*
ávaha, *food.*
ávansa, *man.*
áxak, *two.*

## GLOSSARY

axakyâanich, *only two times (twice).*
áxay-, *to take something from someone.*
axaychákish(rih), *to grab, seize, catch.*
axiich, *child; man's brother's child.*
axmáy, *suddenly.*
axrúhi, *elkhorn purse.*
axvâa, *head.*
axvithíni, *grave, graveyard.*
ay, *to be afraid.*

### ch

Chakíchhaan, *personal name. No mg.*
chánchaaf, *white foam (floats on Klamath River).*
chancháaksur, *smoke-hole (in traditional houses).*
chavúra, *finally.*
chémi, *all right.*
chiimûuch, *lizard.*
chimi, *future tense marker.*
chôora, *let's go!*
chúuphaan, *talker.*
chúuphi, *to talk, to speak; (rooster) to crow.*
chuuphüunish, *to talk with.*

### ee

êem, *Indian doctor, sucking doctor.*
éepaax, *alder bark.*
êer, *to (go) fish. No longer in use—obsolete form.*
êeth, *to carry; (with directionals) to take.*
éethi, *to tell, relate.*

eethríshuk, *to take out.*
êevish, *s. th. to bend over (e.g. a tree).*

### f

fâat, *what? something.*
fáath, *manzanita.*
fâatva, *something, anything.*
fatavêenaan, *name of prayer maker, "medicine man," of the Írahiv, World Renewal Ceremony.*
fíipha, *to die, to be gone, to disappear.*
Firipámyuusa, *Karuk name for Wohtek, a Yurok village, near present day town of Johnson's on Klamath River.*
fúhish, *to believe; to obey (a person).*

### h

hãa, *yes.*
-haan, *one who...*
hâari, *sometimes.*
hámi, *isn't that so?*
-hara, *having.*
hôoy, *where.*
hûut, *how, what.*
hûutva, *somehow, however.*

### i

i-, *you (sg.).*
Íchiraay, *personal name.*
íchunva, *to hide oneself.*
if, *true, really.*
íf, *to grow, to grow up.*
ifápiit, *young woman.*
ífapu, *descendant, e.g.* pananu'ífuth va'ífapuhsas, *our descendants, "our-behind its-having-grown-up."*

ifchuy, *to be crowded.*
ífik, *to pick up (with hands).*
ifuchtîimich, ifuchtîich, *last; the last time: "behind-edge."*
ífuth, *behind, after.*
ifyuk, *to be or go around, to wander.*
ihêer, *to smoke.*
ihrôoha, *wife.*
íhuk, *flower dance, girl's adolescence dance. Íhuk, name of a Spirit Person.*
ihyákuri, *to stick a long object in.*
ihyárihish(rih), *to stand still.*
íihya, *to stand (long object), be.*
îikam, îim, *outside.*
íim, *you (sg.).*
iimkun, *you (pl.).*
iin, *(du. an.) to live, stay, sit, be.*
iin, *to experience something unpleasant, to have something wrong with one. E.g.* hûut ti'iin? *What's the matter with you?*
îin, *by*
iinâak, *indoors, inside a living house.*
iinâakukam. *See* iinâak.
íinva, *forest fire.*
íipma, *(sg.) to arrive there again, go back, return.*
íish, *meat, flesh, body.*
íithka, *feather.*
iithkiri, *put into fire.*
íithra, *(a filled container or its contents) to sit, stand, be; (liquid) to be at rest, to lie.*
ik, *must.*
ikfuk, *to climb, to walk up a mountain.*

ikinayâach, *very straight. Old expression.*
ikiríkir, *name of a headdress worn by obsidian packers.*
ikmaháchraam, *sweat house.*
Iknûumin, *Burrill Peak.*
ikpíhan, *strong.*
ikréemya, *wind.*
ikrih-, *to fish (with a set-net).*
ikrîish(rih), *(sg.) sit down.*
ikriv, *to live, to be.*
ikrívraam, *house, living house.*
iktit, *to undo, unpack.*
iku-, *to lie pointing, to be headed (in some direction).*
ikuuy, *wind to blow on someone.* ikréemyah + ikuuy.
ikvíitha, *to sleep.*
ikvip, *to run (salmon, human beings). Form used when using directionals:* ikvirip-, *to run.*
ikvipvaráyvaan, *the dancer who holds aloft the obsidian blade in the White Deerskin Dance.*
ikviripirópiithva, *to run around.*
ikvíripraa, *to run uphill from downhill.*
ikvíripuni, *to run down.*
ikxáram, *night.*
ikxáramha, *to be dark.*
Ikxaréeyav, *Spirit person, or god.*
Ikxariya-, *compound form of* Ikxaréeyav.
ikxip, *to fly.*
ikxiprúpuk, *to fly through a hole.*
ikxiptánmaahti, *to fly for no reason.*

## GLOSSARY

ikxúrar, *evening.*
ikyaavárihva, *to try.*
ikyav, *to make.*
ikyiv, *to fall.*
imaan, *tomorrow.*
imfir, *to hurt, to burn.*
Imkáanvaan, *personal name. Means "wild sunflower gatherer."*
impaa, *road, trail, path.*
imshírih, *to shine, to sparkle.*
imtananáamnihich, *barely visible.*
imtaránaamha, *to be visible.*
imus-, *to see, look at.*
imúsar, *to go to see, to visit.*
imxup, *to swell.*
imyáaha, *to live.*
imyáahtih, *life.*
inaa, *to go uphill.*
Ínaam, *Clear Creek (a World Renewal ceremony site).*
inhi-, *to tie.*
inhíkan, *a tie, thong. Also,* inhíkar.
inhíkar, *drawstring (the word in common use).*
inirahiram, *where people are living; settlement.*
ípaha, *tree.*
ípahoo, *to continue travelling.*
ípak, *(sg.) to come back, arrive (here) again, to return.*
ipamhi, *to eat.*
ípan, *end, top.*
ípas, *to take, bring (a person).*
ipêer, *to tell, to say to.*
ípi, *bone.*
ipmahóonkoon, *to feel (emotionally).*

ipnaa, *to come back.*
ipsaríshriihva, *(pl.) to carry back.*
ipsháamkiri, *to leave, abandon.*
iptárari< xuus + iptárari, *to be surprised.*
ipúunva, *to rest, take a rest.*
ipuunváram, *a resting-place.*
ipvâaram, *to go back, to go home.*
ipviitshur, *s.o. to paddle off.*
ipvítish, *to beach (canoe).*
ipvôonfuruk, *to come indoors.*
Írahiv, *World Renewal celebration, Fix the Earth ceremony, Indian New Year's.*
irukûuntakoo, *(pl.) to be sitting on [in a row].*
iruvôonupuk, *(du. pl.) to go outdoors.*
íshaha, *water.*
-íshiip, *the best; suffix used to form the superlative.*
ishímfir, *strong, fierce: "flesh-hot."*
íship, *to extend, be in a line.*
Ishipíshrihak, *placename. Means "where the trails comes down to its end," "trailhead-at."*
ishkáakramni, *to jump into a container.*
ishkak, *to jump.*
ishkax, *to be quiet, to think (i.e. to meditate).*
ishkáxish, *to stop (doing something).*
ishkêesh, *Klamath River, river.*
íshki, *quickly.*
ishkúru, *to carry by a looped handle.*

Ishpukatunvêechas, *name of the dentalia necklace. Means "little moneys."*
ishvírip, *Jeffrey pine.*
Ishyâat, *special name for the spring salmon.*
it-, *to look;* it- + *directional.*
itahara-, *ten (compound form).*
itaharâan, *ten times.*
ithâan, *once.*
íthivish(rih), *to be (a specified kind of) "doings" or celebration.*
ithívthaaneen, *the world, the earth.*
ithivthanéen'aachip vákuusrah, *September. Mg. "center-of-the-world-moon."*
ithvuy, *to be named; to cost.*
ithyáa, *fish-dam.*
ithyáruk, ithyarukiruk, *across water, across the river, across a canyon.*
Ithyarukpíhriiv, *name of Spirit Person. Mg. "Across-the-water-widower."*
ithyúuk(iruk), *to one side of the living house; on the other side, across.*
itroopatíshaamnih, *nine.*
itrôovu, *to look upriver.*
itúraayva, *to look around.*
iv, *(sg.) to die.*
iváxra, *dry.*
ivaxráhak, *a dry place.*
ivyíhuk, *(du. pl.) to arrive here.*
ivyíihma, *(du. pl.) to go to, to arrive (going).*
ixrar, *(sg.) to cry, weep; (cat) to meow.*
ixtíivha, *to play (athletic games).*
ixup-, *to cover (several objects); (du. pl.) to lie covering.*
iyâaram, *(du.) to go, leave, to go on to.*
iykar, *to kill, to beat up.*
iyriiv(shav), *to ceremonially or ritually pile rocks.*
iyrúuhriv, *(sg. an.) to lie.*

## k

ka', *upriver.*
-kaam, *big.*
káan, *there.*
kâarim, *bad, bad off, poor, sickly; in-law after death of connecting relative.*
Kaarimchúphaan, *personal name, "bad-talker."*
kachakâach, *bluejay.*
Kahthuxrivishkúruhar, *the Creator spirit. Mg. "upriver-network-sack-carrier."*
kan-, *I (imp. form).*
kana-, *they—me.*
kári, *still.*
kári xás, *and then.*
káru, *and, too.*
káruk, *upstream, upriver.*
káruma, *the fact is.*
Ka'tim'íin, *placename. Mg. "upriver-edge-falls."*
kay, *meaning unknown. Used in phrase* kay kúkuum, *again.*
kêech, *big, large.*
keechíkyav, *sweetheart.*
kêemachkoo, *poor thing.*

## GLOSSARY

kêemish, *monster, poison, danger.*
kéevniikich, *old woman.*
kich, *only, solely.*
kiik-, kii-, *(3p. pl.) you.*
kin-, *you—us.*
kíshvuuf, *angelica root.*
kóo, *all.*
kôokaninay, *everywhere.*
kôomahich, *a little bit.*
kóova, *so much.*
koovúra, *all, all of them.*
kúha, *to be sick (but not seriously), to suffer pain.*
kúkuum, *again.*
kuma-, *it's-, sort of-, kind of-.*
kumá'ii, *because of, the reason why.*
kun-, *they.*
kúna, *or; different.*
kúnish, *sort of, kind of.*
kupa-, *sort of-, kind of-.*
kupánakanakana, *word said at conclusion of a myth.*
kúrat, *California woodpecker.*
kurúthun, *to slide around.*
kushíriv, *a grass that grows along the river.*
kuth, *because of.*
kúuk, *to there, thither.*
kûuntakoo, *(pl.) to sit on.*
kúupha, *to do.*
kûur-, *to sit, to slide (on one's buttocks).*
kûurish(rih), *to sit down.*
kúusra, *sun, and sometimes moon.*
kúyraak, *three.*

## m

ma', *uphill, in the mountains.*
Mâakich, *personal name. Karukacized form of Maggie.*
mah, *to see, to find.*
máharahi, *to follow (as in to learn from).*
máhmaa, *to glimpse intermittently.*
mahxánthuun, *scorpion: "uphill-crawfish."*
mahyáana, *to put in, stuff in.*
manâa, *meaning doubtful.*
máruk, *uphill.*
matêe, *in a moment; wait a moment!*
ma'vánahich, *a little ways uphill.*
mit, *former (remote past tense marker).* míta.
mítva, *previous.*
mu-, *his, her, its.*
múmuh, *dull.*
mûuk, *by means of.*

## n

naa, *to come. (E.g. chimi ôok naa, come here!)*
náa, *I.*
nani-, *my.*
nanu-, *our.*
ni-, *I.*
nîinamich, *small.*
nik, *yet.*
ník áta, *sort of, maybe-maybe not; expression implies doubt.*

## o

ôok, *here.*

# ARARAPÍKVA

## p

pa-, *the.*
pâanpay, *after awhile.*
páathkir, *jump dance headdress.*
  Páathkir, *name of a Spirit Person.*
páathtak, *to throw (-tak, prob. "onto").*
pácheech, *alone, solitary.*
Panámniik, *placename. Orleans. Mg. "flat-place."*
paramsîip(riv). *See* aramsîip.
paratánmaahpa, *to turn back (as on trail).*
pathúvriin, *string of dentalia (not a necklace) used as money.*
páthyuuxriv, *to stick one's legs out in front of oneself.*
pay, *this, that.*
páy nanu'ávahkam, *sky: "this our-above."*
payêem, *now.*
pay'ôok, *right here.*
pihnêefich, *coyote.*
-pîimach, *next to (used usually with possessives).*
piip, *to say.*
píkaruk, *to go to summon a doctor, to go to get a person.*
píkav, *to get a person, to summon a doctor.*
pikrôok, *to remember.*
pikva, *creation story.*
pikváhaan, *a creation story teller.*
pikvaha, *to tell a creation story.*
pikváhahirak, *creation story time.*
pikvas, *a dance feather that stands up: a plume.*

pip, *to bite, (insects) to sting.*
pípasip(rih), *to take someone back.*
pírish, *brush, grass, leaf, plant; medicine (herb); trees, forest.*
pirishkâarim, *grizzly bear.*
pishíich, *first (of several).*
pishpíshi, *yellowjacket.*
piyâaramu, *(du.) to go home.*
piyníknik, *Kick Dance.*
pu...hara, *not...*
púfaat, *nothing. See* púrafaat.
púrafaat, *nothing, gone; not in existence.*
pûuhara, *no.*
púuk, *fog.*
púxay, *emphatically not.*

## r

-riik, *among; place.*

## s

sáak, *arrowhead, flint (obsidian).*
sâam, *downhill (a short distance).*
saamvárak, *to flow from upriver.*
Samnâanak, *placename. Forks of the Salmon. No mg.*
sar-, *to carry, get, bring, take, put (several objects, or a mass of something).*
sára, *bread.*
sáruk, *downhill (a considerable distance); down low on a person's body.*
sav-, *to flow (in a course).*
símsiim, *knife.*
sípnuk'anamahach, *trinket basket. Means "sípnuk-small."*

sípnuk, *storage basket.*
sivríhva, *a location in a traditional living house: in the back.*
sôomkir, *(woman) to offer oneself in marriage.*
súpaah, *day.*
súpaaha, *to be daytime.*
súva, *I hear, you hear, he-she-it-hears.*

## t

ta, *already, by now.*
táat, *mother.*
táay, *lots, many.*
ta'ítam, *so, and, and so.*
táma, *then.*
taníha, *to be spoiled; (persons) to die; (the world) to come to an end.*
-tanmah-, *for no reason.*
tápas, *real*
tapas'ápsuun, *rattlesnake.*
tápkuup, *to like.*
taxrat, *to chip flint.*
taxrátraam, *flintery.*
táyaan, *lots of times.*
típah, *brother.*
turáayva, *to look around, to look for, to seek.*
tûupichas, *little, small (plural).*

## th

thákaariha, *to starve.*
thantak, *to put on (e.g. a rock on pile).*
thantut, *black paint, made of soot and grease.*
thar-, *to lay, put.*

thiina, *to have, to own.*
thítiv, *to hear.*
thivtaap, *War Dance.*
thuxriv, *network sack (netted, open-weave, iris twine bag).*

## u

u-, *he, she, it.*
úhkir, *headband.*
úhraam, *pipe.*
uhyanathêepar, *stories which tell of the first humans.* Mg. *"speech-casting-down."*
uknîi, *indicates a myth is to be recited. Occasionally lengthened to* uknîii.
úkraam, *lake, pond.*
um, *question marker: ?.*
uum, *he, her, it.*
uum, *to arrive.*
uumkun, *they.*
ûumukich, *close-by.*
uunúprav, *to sprout up (plant).*

## v

va-, *its-.*
vaa, *that, thus.*
vâaram, *to go.*
vaas, *blanket.*
Vaatxarákaan, *personal name.* Mg. *"Shouter."*
vápuhirak, *mother's birthplace.*
váramni, *to get in.*
vári, *towards, in the general direction of.*
vásih, *back (body).*
víikar, *basket weaving materials.*
víishriv, *to keep going.*

víitkir, *ridge.*
víitraa, *paddle hither from downstream.*
víitroov, *to paddle upriver.*
vik, *to weave (principally of baskets).*
víkaha, *weaving (i.e. a basket).*
víri, *so*
vishtar, *to like, want (food).*
vishvaan, *belly.*
vit, *to row a canoe, to paddle.*
vítish(rih), *to beach a boat.*
vitívriik, *to row to meet someone.*
vítshur, *to row off.*
vôonupuk, *to leave a house: "to crawl outdoors."*
vôor, *to crawl, creep, move slowly.*
vuhvúh, *to dance the White Deerskin Dance.*
vuhvúha, *White Deerskin Dance.*
vuhvúhiichva, *Imitation Deerskin Dance.*
vúra, *just.*
vúraayva, *to go around, wander.*

## x

xâapish, *Brush Dance. Xâapish, name of a Spirit Person.*
xâat, *even; may.*
xâatik, *"let…"*
xákarari, *on both sides.*
xanchíifich, *frog.*
-xara, *long.*
xára, *long time.*
xás, *then.*
xasík, *then (in the future).*
xávraam, *house-pit.*
xáy, *"let not…! watch out you don't…!"*

Xumkáak, *a village site on Klamath River in Yurok country near mouth.*
xúnutich, *flexible, limber.*
xus, *to think.*
xúseer, *to think (a certain way) about (a person).*
xuun, *acorn soup.*
xuus + êeth, *to take care of.*
xuus + íptarari, *to be surprised.*
xuv-, *to be a gulch, to be a gully.*
xuvúraan, *a hollow (canyon in mountains).*

## y

yâamach, *pretty, nice.*
Yáas'ara, *Humanity, rich man.*
yáavha, *to be in a hurry.*
yakún, *I, you, he saw.*
yánava, *behold.*
yav, *good, well.*
yíchaach, *together, as one.*
yiimúsich, *a little ways off.*
yiiv, *far.*
yíkiha, *sickness.*
yíkihi, *to be (seriously) ill.*
yítha, *one.*
yíthuk, *at some other place.*
yithumásva, *all kinds of.*
yôoram, *at back of living-house.*
yumaaraxatímniim, *giant moth: "dead-man butterfly."*
yúruk, *downstream.*
Yu'tim'îin, *placename. Ike's Falls.*
yûum, yûukam, *(a short distance) downriver.*

# About the Author

Photo of Julian Lang by Lee Brumbaugh

Julian Lang was born in 1951 and grew up in northwestern California. Moving back and forth between Eureka and Somes Bar **(Ka'tim'îin)**, he always lived close to his grandmother, Elizabeth Conrad, a storyteller and fluent speaker of the Karuk language, herself the social center of many of the tribe's traditional elders.

In his senior year of high school, Julian was transferred against his will to Sherman Institute in Riverside, an Indian boarding school, graduating in 1969. He went on to attend College of the Redwoods and California State University at Fullerton, where he studied linguistics, history, music, and eventually theater arts. The birth of his son, Jubilee, interrupted his education. Julian moved to Santa Rosa, and from 1975 to 1979 he directed the Santa Rosa Indian Center.

In 1980 he returned to northwestern California, where he threw himself into Karuk ceremonial and spiritual life. He studied intensively with renowned elders such as Shan Davis, and immersed himself in archival and scholarly material and in the language and music tapes collected generations before by linguists and anthropologists. From one collection of tapes, he learned over two hundred songs, many of which had not been sung for decades.

Julian is founder of the Institute of Native Knowledge, an organization of native people devoted to learning and perpetuating Indian knowledge. He is also an accomplished painter, a writer, and (on occasion) even a performing artist. Generally full of good humor and almost always ready to laugh and enjoy himself, he is also deeply committed to the beauties of the Karuk language, the truths of Karuk culture, and to the Earth. Since his return to northwestern California in 1980 he has been a singer, dancer, and increasingly a leader in the most important of all Karuk ceremonies, the ceremony to Fix the Earth.